Francis Hincks

The Political History of Canada between 1840 and 1855

A Lecture Delivered on the 17th October, 1877

Francis Hincks

The Political History of Canada between 1840 and 1855
A Lecture Delivered on the 17th October, 1877

ISBN/EAN: 9783337072124

Printed in Europe, USA, Canada, Australia, Japan

Cover: Foto ©ninafisch / pixelio.de

More available books at **www.hansebooks.com**

THE
POLITICAL HISTORY OF CANADA

BETWEEN 1840 AND 1855.

A LECTURE

DELIVERED ON THE 17TH OCTOBER, 1877,

AT THE REQUEST OF THE

ST. PATRICK'S NATIONAL ASSOCIATION

WITH COPIOUS ADDITIONS

BY

Hon. Sir FRANCIS HINCKS, P.C., K.C.M.G., C.B.

Montreal :
DAWSON BROTHERS, PUBLISHERS.

1877.

A desire having been expressed that the following lecture—delivered on the 17th October, at the request of the St. Patrick's National Association—should be printed in pamphlet form, I have availed myself of the opportunity of elucidating some branches of the subjects treated of, by new matter, which could not have been introduced in the lecture, owing to its length. I have quoted largely from a pamphlet which I had printed in London in the year 1869, for private distribution, in consequence of frequent applications made to me, when the disestablishment of the Irish Church was under consideration in the House of Commons, for information as to the settlement of cognate questions in Canada, and which was entitled " Religious Endowments in Canada: The Clergy Reserve and Rectory Questions.—A Chapter of Canadian History." The new matter in the pamphlet is enclosed within brackets, thus [ ].

F. HINCKS.

Montreal, October, 1877.

THE POLITICAL HISTORY OF CANADA.

1840 TO 1855.

On Wednesday evening, October 17, a large audience assembled in the Mechanics' Hall to listen to the lecture by Sir Francis Hincks, on the political history of Canada from the Union of Upper and Lower Canada to 1855, delivered under the auspices of the St. Patrick's National Association. The chair was occupied by Mr. Mullarky, the President of the Society, and on the platform were His Worship Mayor Beaudry, Messrs. McMaster, President of the Irish Protestant Benevolent Society, John Kerry, President of the St. George's Society, E. McLelan, President of St. Andrew's Society, McEvenue, President of the Catholic Union, Edward Murphy, M. P. Ryan, M. Donovan, Rafferty, Heffernan, Flannery, Warren, P. Brennan, the Rev. Father Salmon and Capt. Kirwan. Sir Francis Hincks, having been introduced by the Chairman, was most warmly received, and delivered his lecture as follows:—

Mr. President, Ladies and Gentlemen,—When I was honored with an invitation from the St. Patrick's National Association, to deliver them a lecture, it occurred to me that I might, without impropriety, avail myself of the opportunity to carry into effect a long-cherished purpose, and to place on record what circumstances have enabled me to know of the history of Canadian parties during the struggle for, and the ultimate establishment of Parliamentary government, and, during the succeeding years, up to the disruption of the party which had obtained the victory in that memorable contest. Having been myself actively engaged in the struggle both before and after the publication of the celebrated report of the Earl of Durham, I had peculiarly good opportunities of becoming acquainted with the views of those, who took a prominent part in public affairs, not only at the period of the union of the Provinces, but during the succeeding thirteen years. It would obviously be impossible for me, within the limits of a lecture, to give anything that would even merit the designation of an historical sketch, but I venture to hope that it may be in my power to render justice to deceased Canadian statesmen, as well as to give a general idea of the history of the period to which I have referred. It will be my study to speak truthfully and impartially, and to be careful as to the authority on which I make statements which conflict with those of others. It is not my intention to dwell on the events prior to the rebellions in both Provinces in the year 1837. It will be sufficient to remind you that in Lower Canada a large majority of the representatives of the people were in confirmed opposition not only to the Government, but to the Constitution as established by the Imperial Act of 1791. The principal remedial measure advocated by the House of Assembly of Lower Canada was the substitution of an elected for a nominated legislative council. In Upper Canada parties were more equally divided, and the great majority of the Reformers would have been satisfied with the establishment of the existing system of Parliamentary government.

EVENTS BEFORE THE UNION OF 1841.

In the year 1838 the Earl of Durham was appointed Governor-General of the North American Provinces, and High Commissioner to enquire into and to report on their political institutions. The Earl of Durham arrived at Quebec on the 27th of May, and embarked on his return to England on the 1st November, 1838, having been little over five months in the country. He made an elaborate report, which gave entire satisfaction to the Reform party in Upper Canada, and as general dissatisfaction to the party bearing the same designation in Lower Canada. Prior to the rebellion of 1837, the Reform party of Upper Canada had fraternized to some extent with the Lower Canada majority. In a despatch from Sir Francis Head, dated 27th April, 1836, he transmitted to the Secretary of State " the copy of a letter which Mr. Papineau, Speaker of the Assembly of the Lower Province, had addressed to Mr. Bidwell, Speaker of the Assembly of Upper Canada," adding, " I conceive that the traitorous and revolutionary " language it contains as well as the terms in which it speaks of "your Lordship, need no comment." On the 30th August, 1837, Mr. Bidwell had addressed a letter to Dr. O'Callaghan, of Montreal, containing the following passage :—

"Retired from public life, probably for ever, I still look with the deepest interest and sympathy on the efforts of those who are actively contending for the great principles of liberty and good government. Your great and powerful exertions in the cause of liberty and justice I have noticed with admiration and respect, and I look with deep interest on the struggle in Lower Canada between an oppressed and injured people and their oppressors. All hope of justice from the authorities in England seems to be extinguished."

In November, 1835, Mr. William Lyon Mackenzie and Dr. O'Grady, as is stated in the life of the former, visited Quebec "as a deputation from leading and influential Reformers in Upper Canada, to bring about a closer alliance between the Reformers in the two Provinces." It must be evident from the facts just stated, that prior to the events of 1837, there was a cordial understanding between those who were designated as Reformers in the two Provinces.

LORD DURHAM'S REPORT.

In recommending the union of the Provinces the Earl of Durham was chiefly influenced by his conviction that there was an irreconcilable feud between the Canadians of French and British origin, and as he was thoroughly convinced that it was absolutely necessary that the future government of the country should be conducted in accordance with the will of the majority, he came to the conclusion that the two Provinces must be united. I desire to support my statements by unimpeachable authority, and I shall therefore cite Lord Durham's own language:

"Never again will the present generation of French Canadians yield a loyal submission to a British Government; never again will the English population tolerate the authority of a House of Assembly in which the French shall possess or even approximate to a majority."

Wholly erroneous as were Lord Durham's opinions on the subject of the national feud, there can be no doubt that he entertained them honestly, and that they were fully shared by Lord Sydenham, as well as by the Imperial Ministers of the Crown. Lord Durham, however, differed in opinion with those Ministers and with Lord Sydenham on a point of considerable importance, viz., the mode of apportioning the representation. A Canadian historian, Mr. Louis P. Turcotte, whose valuable work, *Le Canada sous l'Union*, I have read with great interest, has fallen into an error on this subject, which I shall venture to correct. Before doing so, permit me to bear my testimony to the value of the work in question, and to express my conviction that any errors which it may contain have been unintentional. Mr. Turcotte's work ought to be translated into English, and I sincerely hope that the author may be encouraged to publish a new edition, and to avail himself of such friendly criticisms as I for one would be ready to submit to him. Referring to Lord Durham's recommendations, Mr. Turcotte observes:—

"For the present he recommended the union of the two Canadas under one government, giving to each the same number of representatives."

Lord Durham himself observes in his report:—

"I am averse to any plan that has been proposed for giving an equal number of representatives to the two Provinces in order to attain the temporary end of outnumbering the French, because I think the same object will be obtained without any violation of the principles of representation, and without any such appearance of injustice in the scheme as would set public opinion both in England and America strongly against it, and because when emigration shall have increased the English population in the upper Province, the adoption of such a principle would operate to defeat the very purpose it is intended to serve. It appears to me that any such electoral arrangement founded on the present Provincial divisions would tend to defeat the purposes of union and perpetuate the idea of disunion."

The foregoing passage deserves to be cited as affording evidence of the sagacity of the Earl of Durham. There is another error of Mr. Turcotte's which I think it desirable to correct, and I may observe that Mr. Withrow has repeated it. Both the historians represent Lord Durham as having recommended a federal union of the British Provinces in his celebrated report, whereas he argued strongly against a federal and in favor of a legislative union. In view of the fact that a few years later Lord Durham's views on responsible government were wholly misunderstood by one of his successors, Sir Charles Metcalfe, it seems desirable to prove by quotations from his report that he clearly understood the principle, the adoption of which he so earnestly recommended. I shall therefore use his own words:—

"It needs no change in the principles of government, no invention of a new constitutional theory to supply the remedy which would, in my opinion, completely remove the existing political disorders. It needs but to follow out consistently the principles of the British Constitution, and introduce into the government of these great colonies those wise provisions, by which alone the working of the representative system can in any country be rendered harmonious and efficient. * * * But the Crown must, on the other hand, submit to the necessary consequences of representative institutions, and if it has to carry on the government in unison with a representative body, it must consent to carry it on by means of those in whom that representative body has confidence. * * * * This change might be effected by a single despatch containing such instructions, or if any legal enactment were requisite, it would only be one that would render it necessary that the official acts of the Governor should be countersigned by some public functionary. This would induce responsibility for every act of the government, and as a natural consequence it would necessitate the substitution of a system of administration by means of competent heads of departments for the present rude machinery of an executive council. * * * I admit that the system which I propose would in fact place the internal government of the colony in the hands of the colonists themselves, and that we should thus leave to them the execution of the laws of which we have long entrusted the making solely to them."

Nothing can be clearer to my mind than the foregoing passages, and yet I shall have to call your attention later to statements in the despatches of Sir Charles Metcalfe which prove either that they were wholly misunderstood or else deliberately misrepresented. I need not dwell further on Lord Durham's recommendations.

LORD SYDENHAM'S GOVERNMENT.

When the Imperial Government decided to carry them into effect, they selected for the office of Governor-General a Cabinet Minister, Mr. Charles Poulett Thomson, who had represented Manchester, one of the most liberal English constituencies, in the House of Commons. Before adverting to the critical period of the Government of Mr. Thomson, afterwards Lord Sydenham, it seems desirable to consider the state of public opinion in the two Provinces. At that time the Reform party consisted of almost the whole French-Canadian population, an equal proportion of the Irish Roman Catholics, and a British minority equal, if not superior in numbers, to the French-Canadian and Irish Catholic Conservatives. The great majority of the British population was included in the Conservative party. I am referring at present to public opinion in Lower Canada. It is stated in Turcotte's history that the French-Canadians of Quebec and Three Rivers, supported by their clergy and a considerable number of influential English, petitioned against the Union, and in favor of the Constitution of 1791. The number of signatures was 40,000. A meeting was likewise held in Montreal, and an address carried against the Union on the proposition of Mr. Lafontaine. The majority of the British population were decidedly favorable to the principle of the Union Act. In Upper Canada the Reformers warmly approved of the chief recommendations of Lord Durham's report, which induced a considerable number of the old opponents of Responsible Government to announce their adhesion to that principle. The bulk of the Conservative party avowed their opposition to Lord Durham's views, and a select committee of the House of Assembly made an elaborate report against them. The opposition of that party was not only directed against Responsible Government, but likewise against the Union, as evidenced by a joint address from the Legislative Council and House of Assembly. Such was the state of public opinion when Mr. Thomson assumed the Government, charged specially to endeavor to procure the assent of the respective Legislatures to the re-union of the Provinces. The Constitution having been suspended in Lower Canada, and the Special Council being composed chiefly of members of the British party, no difficulty was experienced in obtaining the assent of the only Legislature in existence in Lower Canada. In Upper Canada the Reformers supported Mr. Thomson with great cordiality, and as he claimed and obtained the support of the officials, he was enabled to carry his measure by a sufficient majority. The Conservative minority desired to obtain a larger representation for Upper Canada, and other conditions to which the Governor was unable to assent. Although in the discussion which took place in the British House of Commons on Lord Durham's report, Lord John Russell had announced that the Government could not concur in the recommendation to establish Responsible Government, His Lordship later in the year wrote a despatch, dated 16th October, 1839, in which he directed that the principal officers of the Crown, particularizing the Secretary, the Receiver-General, the Attorney and Solicitor-General, should be informed that hereafter their offices were to be held strictly during pleasure, and that they would be called on to retire whenever public policy might render such a step advisable. This celebrated despatch was published, and about the same time the Governor, in reply to an address from the Assembly requesting copies of despatches on the subject of Responsible Government, declined furnishing the despatches, but informed them that "he had received Her Majesty's commands to administer the Government in accordance with the well-understood wishes and interests of the people, and to pay to their feelings, as expressed by their representatives, the deference that is justly due to them." The despatch of 16th October and the reply to the Assembly were generally accepted by the Reformers as an assurance that Lord Durham's recommendation would be acted on. It is important, in order to understand the history of the period, to note the changes in parties consequent on the determination of the Imperial Government to give effect to Lord Durham's recommendation to reunite the Provinces. Mr. Thomson was in an exceptional position. He was virtually an autocrat in Lower Canada, and, owing to the position of parties, almost as powerful in Upper Canada. He had divided the Conservative party in that Province, and in addition to a Conservative minority, had as his supporters the Reformers of Upper Canada and the British or Conservative party of Lower Canada, while the opposition to his Government consisted of the French-Canadians and their British contingent, and the majority of the Conservatives of Upper Canada, parties having no sympathy whatever with each other. The tone of the press affords a good indication of the state of feeling. The Montreal *Herald* declared that Lord Durham's report was "the most luminous, comprehensive and best arranged "document on the affairs of the colonies which has ever been "submitted to the British Parliament." The Montreal *Gazette* styled it " a document of great research, noted impartial- "ity, and fraught with just conclusions with regard to the " best interests and the ultimate welfare of these Provinces." I have already noticed the strong opposition of the French-Canadians. The Toronto *Patriot* referred to " the conduct of the froward nobleman and his knot of loafer-secretaries and hangers-on," and declared that "the Ministers have made for themselves a pretty kettle of fish by employing Jacobins and loafers to regulate the affairs of a Conservative and loyal people." This journal was the exponent of the views of the Conservative party of Upper Canada, which had been in the ascendant up to the time of Mr. Thomson's assumption of the Government. The *British Colonist* and *Christian Guardian* may fairly be considered as representing the views of the moderate Conservatives, who cordially supported the union policy of Mr. Thomson, and who were not disinclined to accept Responsible Government; indeed, Mr. Henry John Boulton, Mr. Hamilton Merritt and Mr. Adam Fergusson gave their formal adhesion to that principle after the publication of Lord Durham's report. I was at that time editor of the Toronto *Examiner*, and had been contending for Responsible Government against almost the entire press of Upper Canada during the whole period of Lord Durham's government. The *Examiner* gave a cordial support to Lord Durham's recommendations, and to the Union scheme of Mr. Thomson. In February, 1840, after the close of the session of the Upper Canada Legislature, a vacancy having occurred on the Bench, Mr. Attorney-General Hagerman was appointed Judge, Mr. Solicitor-General Draper Attorney-General, and Mr. Robert Baldwin, the most conspicuous member of the Reform party was invited by Mr. Thompson to fill the office of Solicitor-General.

THE LATE ROBERT BALDWIN.

All the circumstances of Mr. Baldwin's acceptance of a seat in the Executive Council under Sir Francis Head four years previously, and his subsequent resignation being well known, the offer of office was a virtual declaration to the country that the Government under the Union would be conducted in accordance with the wishes of the majority. Mr. Baldwin's political friends were at the time supporters of the Government, and he did not feel justified in refusing the offer of office. His opinion, concurred in by his political friends, was that until after the elections under the Union Act, it could not be expected that the Governor-General could form an efficient administration for the United Province. The Governor had encountered warm opposition from the French Canadians, and there can be no doubt that his belief was that, by the Union of the British party in Lower Canada with the moderate Conservatives and Reformers in Upper Canada, a working majority would be obtained in the new House of Assembly. Mr. Baldwin and his friends were of opinion that the natural combination of parties would be the Reformers of Upper and Lower Canada, the latter consisting chiefly of French-Canadians, with whom the Irish Catholics were at that time allied. I cannot introduce the name of Mr. Baldwin without expressing my deep sense of his great merits as a statesman and a patriot. Many of his contemporaries have passed away, but there are still some survivors of those who fought the great battle for Constitutional Government under the leadership of Robert Baldwin. I cannot forbear referring here to a letter which I received a few months ago from an old and valued friend who had been reading an historical lecture which was delivered about that time by the Hon. Mr. Laurier. He wrote as follows :—

" If he (Mr. Laurier) knew as much as you and I do about the establishment of Constitutional Government, I think he would at least have mentioned the name of Robert Baldwin in his lecture. Whilst many of the advanced liberals of that day were seeking to rid the country of the irresponsible mode of conducting the Government, which had become intolerable, by advocating elective institutions, Robert Baldwin, from the first contended that the English Constitutional system of responsibility afforded the true solution of our difficulties. How zealously and disinterestedly he laboured to save his country from the crushing effects of a rash and unsuccessful resort to physical force—with what contempt and indifference he treated the slanders of his political opponents —how perseveringly he pursued the wise and prudent course he had marked out for himself until the complete establishment of responsible government was triumphantly attained, no one knows better than you, and you, as his colleague, also know the enormous amount of labor which he bestowed on the establishment and perfecting of the municipal system and other kindred legislative measures which he considered necessary to solidify and make more perfect the government of the country under that system which he had so long laboured to establish. It seems to me that justice has not been done to the memory of Robert Baldwin, and there is no man now living who knew him as you did, who can testify in his favor as you can. I hope you will be able to do something to keep alive the memory of our old friend and leader, for it seems to me he is almost forgotten by the new men who now fill the seats of power and occupy positions of prominence."

It no doubt appears strange that any one acquainted with

Canadian history could lecture thereon without bearing testimony to the labors of Robert Baldwin,—but Mr. Laurier, although professing to review the history of the Liberal party in this country, seems to have been of the opinion that he could do so satisfactorily by ignoring the existence of the Upper Canada section of that party, and by keeping in abeyance the political questions which led to its disruption, although several of them were deeply interesting to the people of Lower Canada. It is to be regretted that no one has undertaken to publish a life of Robert Baldwin, but I entertain no doubt that his memory has been, and will continue to be, held in high esteem by his countrymen. Unfortunately, owing to his having had to place himself in opposition to Sir Francis Head, to Lord Sydenham and to Lord Metcalfe, his character has been aspersed in books that are to be found in most English libraries. The most offensive of the attacks on Mr. Baldwin's character is to be found in the life of Lord Metcalfe by the late Sir John William Kaye, one of the worst class of biographies, the author apparently considering it his duty to cast the vilest imputations on all who differed in opinion with his hero, of whom he writes in terms of the most fulsome adulation. Sir John Kaye was never in Canada, had never seen Mr. Baldwin, and must have derived his information either from Lord Metcalfe himself or from his immediate dependents. He commences the description of his character by alleging that he was "the son of a gentleman of Toronto, of "American descent, who had formerly been a member of what is "called the 'Family Compact.' The elder Baldwin had quar- "relled with his party, and with the characteristic bitterness of a "renegade had brought up his son in extremest hatred of his old "opponents and had instilled into him the most liberal opinions." It would be difficult to crowd a greater number of errors into the same space. The worthy and highly esteemed father of Robert Baldwin, Dr. William Warren Baldwin, was an Irishman, a native of the County of Cork, and was never a member of the "Family Compact," nor did he ever hold other than the most liberal opinions. Sir Francis Head, certainly not a partial judge, describes him as "rather more ultra in his theory of reform than "his son, a gentleman of very large property, who is respected "for his moral character, and who had also been recommended by "my predecessor for a seat in the Legislative Council." Neither the doctor nor his son entertained bitter feelings against their opponents, and although firm in their adherence to cherished political opinions they were both highly and universally respected. Sir John Kaye asserts that Robert Baldwin "seemed to delight in strife." A very brief reference to his public career will be the most satisfactory refutation of this statement. At the early age of 24 he was elected, in 1828, member for the town of York, now the city of Toronto, on the reform interest. He is said by Withrow in his History of Canada, " during the entire course " of his public life to have commanded the esteem of both political " parties. His personal integrity, his legal ability and his singu- " lar moderation enabled him, as has been admirably said, to lead " his country through a great constitutional crisis into an era of " larger and more matured liberty." In 1830, two years after his election, there was a sudden dissolution of the Liberal House of Assembly on the ground of the demise of King George the Fourth. The Reformers were defeated, and Mr. Baldwin withdrew entirely from politics for about six years. In 1836 he was invited by Sir Francis Head to become a member of the Executive Council. Sir Francis Head's own despatch, dated February, 1836, is a complete refutation of Kaye's unfounded accusation. He writes to Lord Glenelg :—" After making every enquiry in my power, I became " of opinion that Mr. Robert Baldwin, advocate, a gentleman al- " ready recommended to Your Lordship by Sir John Colborne for " a seat in the Legislative Council, was the first individual I " should select, being highly respected for his moral character, " being moderate in his politics, and possessing the esteem and " confidence of all parties." The foregoing character was obtained by Sir Francis Head, not from Mr. Baldwin's political friends, but from his opponents, one of whom (Chief Justice Robinson) is specially referred to. Mr. Baldwin held the office of Executive Councillor in 1836 for about three weeks, he and his colleagues having resigned, as he did nearly eight years afterwards, when he found that the Governor was determined to conduct public affairs without the advice of his known and responsible Councillors. A dissolution of the Assembly having taken place owing to its rupture with Sir Francis Head, consequent on the resignation of Mr. Baldwin and his colleagues, and the Government having been successful, Mr. Baldwin accepted the verdict of the country, and again withdrew entirely from public life, declining to attend meetings or to be a party to the agitation which culminated in the rebellion of 1837. He continued in retirement until he was again invited by Lord Sydenham to accept the office of Solicitor-General at the time when the union of the two provinces was about to be consummated. This is the man who was pronounced by Lord Metcalfe's biographer to have been possessed of "unbounded arrogance and self-conceit;" to have been "serving his own ends by "the promotion of his ambition, the gratification of his vanity or "his spite." It is to be regretted that Canada's most illustrious statesman is chiefly known to English readers by the character given to him by Sir Francis Head and by the authors of the lives of Lords Sydenham and Metcalfe. I have digressed from my subject in order to pay a merited tribute to the character of one for whom from the period of my first acquaintance, about 45 years ago, I entertained the most profound veneration, which was not in the least abated, during the period in 1841 and 1842, when I was temporarily estranged from him, under circumstances to which I shall have occasion to advert.

SIR LOUIS LAFONTAINE AND DR. TRACY.

This is a convenient opportunity to do justice to another highly valued friend, the late Sir Louis Lafontaine. The great French-Canadian statesman was of course better known in Montreal than Mr. Baldwin, and many are living in our midst, both old supporters and old opponents. I can hardly believe that there is a single individual in the ranks of either party who would admit that Kaye was correct in attributing to Sir Louis Lafontaine "indecision and infirmity of purpose." I can declare, for my own part, that I never met a man less open to such an imputation. It is true that Kaye acknowledges that "his better qualities were natural to him; his worse were the growth of circumstances. * * * He was a just and honourable man; his motives were above all suspicion." Strange, however, that Kaye could believe that such a man could be elevated to the leadership of an "important and united party," without any particular fitness, and "by the force rather of his moral than his intellectual qualities." When lecturing under the auspices of the St. Patrick's National Association, I cannot omit paying a just tribute to the memory of one who took an active part in the great struggle for Constitutional Government, at the most gloomy period of the contest; but who did not live to share in the rewards of victory. I allude to our distinguished countryman, Dr. Tracy, who was cut off in the prime of life, and in the full vigour of his faculties. I had not the advantage of Dr. Tracy's personal acquaintance, but, from the period of my first residence in Montreal, in 1844, I and my family were privileged to enjoy the friendship of his sister, Mrs. Charles Wilson, who still survives, honoured and beloved by the whole Irish population for her intellectual, as well as her many amiable qualities. When in better health than she has of late years enjoyed, she was the most active supporter of every project suggested for the benefit of the Irish population. Those who visit the cemetery are reminded by the beautiful monument, erected to the memory of Dr. Tracy, of his patriotic services to the country of his adoption.

POLITICAL COMBINATIONS AFTER THE UNION.

I must revert to the period of our history when a political alliance was formed between Mr. Lafontaine and Mr. Baldwin, which was only dissolved when they retired from public life, about the same time, in the year 1851. During the year 1840, in the early part of which Mr. Baldwin accepted office, there were no political events of any importance. There were some communications between the leaders of the Reform party in Upper Canada and the principal French Canadians, the object having been to ascertain how far it would be possible for the Reformers of the two Provinces to act in concert. The Lower Canadian Liberals were unable to accept the Union Act, and were consequently in direct opposition to the Government, in which the Upper Canada Reformers very generally professed confidence. Unfortunately for the reputation of Lord Sydenham, there was not a fair representation of Lower Canada in the first Union Parliament, and for this, to some extent at least, he must be held personally responsible. In the Union Bill, as originally introduced by Lord John Russell, it was provided that "the incorporated cities of Quebec and Montreal" should be represented; but in the Act, as finally passed, a clause was introduced empowering the Governor to define the boundaries of the several cities and towns named in the Act. Under this authority, Lord Sydenham, by a stroke of his pen, disfranchised two-thirds of the inhabitants of Montreal and Quebec, inhabiting the suburbs, and secured the return of members pledged to support his government. Some of the counties, but notably Terrebonne, for which Mr. Lafontaine, the Lower Canadian leader, was a candidate, were carried by violence; armed bands of non-residents having been marched to a polling place fixed at a remote corner of the county, at a distance from the centres of the population. The consequence of this policy was the increased hostility of the French Canadians to the Government. On the meeting of the Legislature it was found that the Reformers of Lower Canada, instead of having a majority, as had been fully anticipated of nearly twenty, were only about equal to the number of their opponents. In Upper Canada, the Conservative members who acknowledged Sir Allan McNab as their leader, were few in number, while the Reformers had a very decided majority. On the meeting of Parliament, Mr. Baldwin summoned a meeting of the members of the Liberal party from both sections of the now united Province. The chief object of the meeting was to ascertain whether the Reformers of the two sections were satisfied with the composition of the Government, and there was almost an unanimous declaration of want of confidence. Mr. Baldwin thereupon recommended to the Governor a reconstruction of the administration; and, on his advice being rejected, resigned. Mr. Baldwin was severely censured by his late colleagues and their friends for the course of proceeding which he adopted, a course which no one would have more readily condemned than Mr. Baldwin himself, if the administration had been formed in the usual way. The union of the two Provinces, the members of which were not even personally acquainted, caused an abnormal condition of affairs. Mr. Baldwin had been invited by the Governor to accept a seat in the Executive Council in February, 1841, in the following terms:—

"I am called upon to name an Executive Council for this Province without delay, which at present will be composed exclusively of the chief officers of the Government, and I have therefore included your name in the list."

Mr. Baldwin wrote to Lord Sydenham in reply, regarding the composition of the Council:—

"With respect to those gentlemen, Mr. Baldwin has himself an entire want of political confidence in all of them except Mr.

Dunn, Mr. Harrison, and Mr. Daly. * * * He deems it a duty which he owes to the Governor-General at once to communicate his opinion that such arrangement of the administration will not command the support of Parliament."

Such language could admit of but one construction—Mr. Baldwin plainly indicated his intention, when the proper time came, to require a reconstruction of the Cabinet; but, pending the meeting of the Legislature, was unwilling to create embarrassment to the Governor by any premature action. He, however, did not conceal from his colleagues his want of political confidence in them. If the Governor or his colleagues had been of opinion that Mr. Baldwin's retention of his seat in the Council, under the circumstances, was objectionable, they could have required his immediate resignation. His own opinion was that the assembling together of the newly-elected representatives of the reunited Provinces, on the occasion of the meeting of Parliament, was the proper time for action; and that, had he taken any more energetic step than he did, he would have laid himself open to the charge of causing unnecessary embarrassment to the Governor-General. He had, shortly after his appointment to the office of Solicitor-General, February, 1840, written a letter, which was published at the time, in which he stated:—

"I distinctly avow that in accepting office I consider myself to have given a public pledge that I have a reasonably well grounded confidence that the Government of my country is to be carried on in accordance with the principles of Responsible Government which I have ever held. My position politically is certainly peculiar, but its peculiarity has arisen out of the position in which the present Parliament placed the Governor-General, themselves and the country by the course they chose to adopt during the last session, and it is therefore right that it should be distinctly understood that I have not come into office by means of any coalition with the Attorney-General or with any others now in the public service, but have done so under the Governor-General and expressly from my confidence in him."

It is to be borne in mind that Mr. Baldwin professed confidence in some of his colleagues, and his advice was that the Government should be reconstructed very much as was done about a year later under the Government of Sir Charles Bagot.

[I think it desirable to quote here at some length, from a new work, "The Irishman in Canada," Mr. Baldwin's own explanation of the circumstances attending his acceptance and resignation of a seat in the Executive Council in the year 1841.

He admitted he was responsible to the bar of public opinion. The course which he had taken in accepting office on the proclamation of the Union had been condemned. It had, however, been forgotten, that he was not, at the time, in the position of one out of the Administration, and then, for the first time, invited to join it. The Head of the Government, the heads of departments in both Provinces, and the country itself were in a position almost anomalous. That of the Head of the Government was one of great difficulty and embarrassment. While he felt bound to protect himself against misapprehensions as to his views and opinions, he also felt bound to avoid, as far as possible, throwing any difficulties in the way of the Governor-General. At the time he was called to a seat in the Executive Council, he was already one of those public servants, the political character newly applied to whose offices made it necessary for them to hold seats in that Council. Had he, on being called to take that seat, refused to accept it, he must of course have left office altogether, or have been open to the imputation of objecting to an arrangement for the conduct of public affairs, which had always met with his most decided approbation. In either case, what a position he would have been placed in. How triumphantly would those who condemned him for accepting that seat, have then denounced him as one utterly impracticable, if not absolutely factious.

What doubts and fears would have been raised. No step, as Baldwin did not hesitate to say—without assuming any importance, other than such as the connection of his humble name with the great principle of Responsible Government had, in the public eye, attributed to him—could have been taken which would have been more calculated to produce distrust and alarm. It was under a deep sense of the responsibility which he would incur in taking such a step, that he had come to the conclusion that his course was to accept the seat to which the Head of the Government had called him. In the peculiar position in which he was placed, coupled with his well-known political opinions, either as to men or measures, neither the Head of the Government, nor the members of the Council who now condemned him, would have had any just ground of complaint against him. He had taken office originally with a full avowal of his principles, and of his want of political confidence in certain gentlemen. He had not rested satisfied with that, but had, in order to prevent any possible misconception, explicitly declared those opinions, both to the Head of the Government and to those honorable gentlemen, previous to his acceptance of a seat in the Executive Council.

On the 13th February, 1841, Lord Sydenham had written to him that he was called upon to name an Executive Council for this Province without delay, which, for the present, would be composed exclusively of the chief officers of the Government, and that he had therefore inserted his name in the list. Did not that note, argued Baldwin, show that the Governor himself looked forward to such changes as the calls of public opinion might afterwards demand, " more particularly when attention to such calls formed the very basis of the new principle to which allusion had been so often made?" A few days afterwards, on the 18th or 19th of the same month, he had replied that he had to acknowledge the receipt of the Governor-General's note, informing him that His Excellency had done him the honour of calling him to the Executive Council of the United Province; that he was still ignorant, except from rumour, who the other councillors were to be; that assuming that the gentlemen to whom rumour had assigned seats in the new Council were those who His Excellency felt it necessary should "at present" compose it, such an administration would not command the support of Parliament; that he had an entire want of political confidence in all of them, except Mr. Dunn, Mr. Harrison, and Mr. Daly, and that had he reason to suppose that the generally understood political principles and views of the other gentlemen of the Council were those upon which the Government was to be administered, it would be his duty respectfully to decline continuing to hold office under them.

At such a critical moment, however, he shrank from everything that would be in the least calculated to embarrass the Government. He, therefore, would not feel justified in refusing the place to which he had been appointed. His silent acceptance of office might, however, be misinterpreted by the members of the Council, in whom he had no confidence, as an expression of his confidence. He would take it for granted there could be no objection to his making them acquainted with his sentiments.

He accordingly addressed letters to those gentlemen, informing them of his utter want of political confidence in them. Could he have done more to prevent misconception? True, he might have retired from the Government at the time; but so might the gentlemen to whom he objected, who were precisely in the same position as he was. If he did not take that course, it was because he was impelled to a contrary one by a strong sense of duty. He had felt, as he took it for granted they had done, that the verdict of the country was to decide whether their political views or his were most in accordance with the wishes and interests of the people. The charge of not having interchanged with his temporary colleagues those communications which might have led to a correct estimate of the respective political opinions of each, was no charge at all, except upon the supposition that he had entered into a coalition with them. Without that ground of complaint, all the charge amounted to was that he had not acted inconsistently with his already avowed opinion concerning them, and misled them, by a show of confidence, into a belief that his previously expressed opinions had been modified; or it resolved itself into a repetition, in a new shape, of the first charge of accepting the office of Executive Councillor at all, to which he had already given a sufficiently satisfactory answer. Those gentlemen of the Administration in whom he had felt and avowed political confidence, knew that he had communicated with them in the fullest and frankest manner upon every topic connected with the state of the country, and upon none more fully than that involved in the subject of the present discussion. The third charge was, that he had not, at an earlier period, tendered that advice, upon the rejection of which he had felt himself called upon to resign. It was hard that he was, on the one hand, accused of precipitancy; and on the other of delay. But when the circumstances in which he was p'aced were fairly considered; when it was remembered that, from the time of his appointment to the time of his proceeding to Montreal, he had been actively engaged, first with the Upper Canada elections, and more particularly the contest for Hastings and the City of Toronto, and afterwards with the duties of his office of Solicitor-General as public prosecutor on the Home Circuit; that he had not only expressly communicated to the Head of the Government, at the time of accepting the seat in the Executive Council, his expectations of the result of the elections then about to come off, but had never concealed his opinion that those anticipations had been realised; that he had, when in Lower Canada, the advantage of seeing only a portion of the Reform members who had been returned to the United Parliament, and had not had an opportunity of ascertaining how far the Reformers of both sections of the Province were prepared to act together—a course on their parts which he had always deemed of the most vital importance to the best interests of his country; when these circumstances were considered, he felt convinced that every dispassionate man in the community would acquit him of any unnecessary delay in tendering his advice to Lord Sydenham.]

POSITION OF PARTIES IN 1841.

The effect of Mr. Baldwin's resignation was to place him in opposition to his old colleagues, all of whom, Reformers as well as Conservatives, retained office, and although frequently defeated, owing to combinations of parties having little sympathy with each other, the Government succeeded in getting through the session without serious difficulty. There were at least five if not six parties in the House, three from each Province. In Upper Canada there were, 1st, the old Conservative party led by Sir Allan

Macnab; 2nd, the Ministerial party composed chiefly of Reformers, with a few Moderate Conservatives, under the leadership of Mr. Attorney-General Draper and Mr. Secretary Harrison; 3rd, the Reformers who followed the lead of Mr. Baldwin, numbering six to eight. In Lower Canada there were—1st, the Reformers of French and Irish origin with their allies of the British party, led by Mr. Morin, Mr. Neilson and Mr. Aylwin; 2nd, The British party, including the Conservative French-Canadians and Irish elected to support Lord Sydenham's policy, and almost uniformly doing so that session, although several of them had a decided bias in favor of a Liberal policy, while others were as decidedly Conservative. I may mention the names of two representative men, both deservedly respected, and both at the time members for the City of Montreal, the Hon. Geo. Moffatt and Benjamin Holmes. A year later those gentlemen were completely separated as to party connection, the former being as decidedly on the Conservative as the latter was on the Liberal side. At the period to which I am referring, both were supporters of the Administration. The division lists of the session of 1841 cannot fail to strike any one acquainted with the state of parties as extraordinary. Mr. Baldwin, on several occasions voted with considerable majorities in opposition to the Government, while as frequently he was in insignificant minorities. There was a decided tendency towards a coalition with the Reformers of French origin on the part of Sir Allan MacNab and the Upper Canada Conservatives. The Ministerial strength lay in the support which it received from the British party of Lower Canada, and from the majority of the Upper Canada Reformers. On more than one occasion, especially the election bill, the latter followed Mr. Baldwin's lead, and the bill was carried against the Government in the Commons, but was thrown out by the Legislative Council. There was a great contest over the Municipal Bill, which was the most important measure of the session, and it was on one occasion saved from defeat by the casting vote of the Chairman of the Committee of the Whole. Sir Allan McNab and his Conservative friends, and Mr. Neilson and many Lower Canadians were wholly opposed to municipal institutions, while Mr. Baldwin was desirous of amending the Government bill so as to make it more Liberal. The Government announced its determination on what I thought at the time, and still think, justifiable grounds, to withdraw the bill, if any important amendment were carried, and on this, as on several other occasions as the session advanced, I considered it my duty to support the Government. I found on better acquaintance that I had no opinions in common with Mr. Neilson, who, from his age and experience, had great influence in the councils of the Opposition party, and I found several of the Lower Canada British members as thoroughly Liberal as I could wish. The resolutions recognizing Responsible Government were carried with only seven dissentients, four from Upper and three from Lower Canada. Mr. Neilson did not vote, but he was an avowed opponent of the principle, and before another year had expired was openly in the Conservative ranks. Towards the end of the session Lord Sydenham met with the accident which caused his premature death. He was succeeded, after an interval of a few months, by Sir Charles Bagot. In June, 1842, I was invited to accept the office of Inspector-General, and as I had considered it my duty to support the principal measures of the Government during the preceding session, and as I felt bound, under existing circumstances, to cast my lot with those with whom I had entered into alliance, I did not hesitate to do so. All my leading supporters in the County of Oxford testified their approbation of my conduct by supporting me on the occasion of my re-election.

THE SECOND SESSION OF THE UNION.

About three months afterwards the second session of the First Parliament of United Canada was opened by Sir Charles Bagot. There was no material difference in the state of parties, although the Opposition had gained a few seats, and had been much strengthened by the return of Mr. Lafontaine, the leader of the French Canadians, for the North Riding of York, in Upper Canada, Mr. Baldwin who had had a double return, having vacated that seat, and having strongly recommended his Lower Canadian ally to the electors. The address in answer to the speech having been moved in due course, Mr. Baldwin proposed in amendment a vote of want of confidence. Meantime, negotiations had been commenced for a reconstruction of the administration. It cannot be denied that they were very clumsily managed. A written proposal was made to Mr. Lafontaine by the Governor, which he felt himself unable to accept, and in the course of the debate the Governor's letter was read by Mr.

Attorney General Draper, who was able to make out a strong case for himself. He acknowledged with great frankness that he had at one time been prejudiced against the French-Canadians, but declared that the experience of the previous session had removed all his objections to acting with them. He admitted the necessity of introducing into the Government gentlemen possessing their confidence, and as he was aware that under existing circumstances they could not take office without Mr. Baldwin, he stated that he had more than once tendered his own resignation, in order that his office might be offered to that gentleman. There is no doubt that the leaders of the Opposition, Messrs. Lafontaine and Baldwin, were desirous of forcing the Ministry to resign, in the expectation that one of them would have been called on to form a new administration, and it is not improbable that if the Ministers had been weak enough to yield, such a result might have ensued. The Ministers, however, were firm on all essential points. They yielded so far on the proposed pensions to Mr. Ogden, the Attorney General, whose office had been offered to Mr. Lafontaine, and to Mr. Davidson, the Commissioner of Crown Lands, as to consent that their new colleagues and their friends should vote as they pleased, but Mr. Turcotte has fallen into an error in stating in his history that they retained their seats on the condition of conforming to the policy of their new chiefs. No such stipulation, nor any other, except on the subject of the pension vote, was proposed.

[As it became my duty, owing to my official position, to propose the pension vote, and as there seems to exist some misapprehension as to a proceeding which I can readily understand seems extraordinary to those unacquainted with circumstances, I think it desirable to offer some explanation regarding it. Prior to the introduction of responsible government, the principal offices were in practice held during good behavior, precisely as the non-political offices, such as deputy heads of departments, are now held both in Canada and England. There was, of course, a difficulty in subjecting such incumbents of offices to political responsibility. In Nova Scotia, if I am not mistaken, one, if not more, of that class was pensioned. Lord Sydenham had induced Mr. Secretary Daly, Mr. Attorney General Ogden, and Mr. Solicitor-General Day in Lower Canada, to find seats in parliament. The Commissioner of Crown Lands, Mr. Davidson, who was an old public servant, declined entering political life, but his office was considered one which should be made political. To have simply dismissed such a man, who had taken no part in politics, because his office was wanted, would have been an act of cruelty, exactly similar to the dismissal of any non-political officer under our present government without his having committed a fault of any kind. So little did Mr. Davidson know of the political negotiations, that his office had been conferred on another before he even knew that any change was thought of. Mr. Ogden's case was not quite so strong, because he had been returned as a member, and had virtually accepted the political position. Nevertheless, he had accepted the office when it was non-political, and was on leave of absence when the changes took place. If length of service was an element in the case, his claim was much stronger than Mr. Day's, whose tenure of office had been short in comparison with Mr. Ogden's. During the interval between the sessions of 1841 and 1842, Mr. Day was appointed to the Bench, of which for many subsequent years he was an ornament. I believe that under different circumstances neither Mr. Lafontaine nor Mr. Baldwin would have disputed the propriety of awarding pensions to two old public servants deprived of their offices owing to the introduction of a new principle of government. I at all events cordially concurred with my colleagues in thinking that the proposed pensions should be granted. I can quite understand the reluctance of Mr. Lafontaine to accept office on the condition that he was to provide a pension for the previous incumbent. The point was not one on which an important political arrangement could be upset. It was agreed that the pension question should be an open one. When I proposed it to the House, Messrs. Lafontaine and Baldwin were absent, having to be re-elected after acceptance of office, and an amendment to postpone the consideration of the question until the following session was carried on a division. During the recess an opportunity occurred of conferring on Mr. Davidson the office of Collector of Customs at Hamilton, which he readily accepted instead of a pension, and the new ministers willingly consented to get rid of the difficulty in that way. Mr. Ogden's case was disposed of by the Imperial Government, which gave him the appointment of Attorney-General to the Isle of Man. Mr. Daly's case created embarrassment a year later. He ought, as an old public officer, to have been pensioned at the Union. He was forced into political life, for which he had no aptitude, and when the Metcalfe crisis took place he retained his office. When he was forced to retire in 1848 he was provided for by the Imperial Government. Mr. Dunn and Mr. Sullivan, who were in the same position, resigned with their colleagues in 1843, the former returning to England and receiving no compensation for the loss of an office conferred on him many years previously as nonpolitical, and the latter resuming the practice of a profession which he had abandoned for a non-political office understood at the time to be permanent. The result was that the change from non-political to political heads of departments in Upper and Lower Canada was accomplished without a single Canadian pension, Mr. Ogden and Mr. Daly having both been compensated by employment under the Imperial Government.]

In giving a list of the Ministers, Mr. Turcotte places Mr. Lafontaine's name at the head as "First Minister," exactly as it was properly placed in 1848. In 1842 Mr. Lafontaine, Mr. Baldwin, Mr. Morin, Mr. Aylwin, and Mr. Small became members of the old Government, six members of which retained their offices and their precedence, without concessions of any kind. Mr. Withrow is still more inaccurate. He states that even prior to the reconstruction " the principle of double majority, as it was called, was introduced." And why introduced? To counteract, he says, " the dominant influence " of the French members, who, numbering twenty-four, " held the balance of power." Now, it so happens that the French Canadian members, instead of holding the balance of power, never had so little influence as during the first session of the First Parliament. This was owing to the disfranchisement of Montreal and Quebec, and to the elections carried by violence. The balance of power was held by the Reformers of Upper Canada, who generally supported the Government, but occasionally divided with Mr. Baldwin. A Government of " double majority," instead of counteracting the influence of the French Canadians, would have been the means of securing it. Elsewhere, when referring to Mr. Baldwin's resignation in 1854, Withrow asserts that " since the union, successive Ministers had succeeded in carrying their measures by a majority from each Province." The fact is that during the whole of the second Parliament the Government was sustained by a majority from Upper Canada acting with a Lower Canada minority. Mr. Baldwin's resignation is stated to have taken place "in obedience to this principle," but if a principle was at stake, all Mr. Baldwin's Upper Canada colleagues should likewise have resigned, and yet it was his own earnest request that they should not do so. Mr. Baldwin resigned because he was abandoned by almost the entire legal profession of Upper Canada, on a measure, the Court of Chancery, which he had himself carried through the Legislature, and for which he held himself personally responsible. I cannot make this allusion to that measure without recording my opinion that the attacks frequently made against the late Chancellor Blake as having promoted the Chancery Act in order to provide a place for himself, are most unjust. Mr. Blake was not a member of the Administration, and Mr. Baldwin himself was the author of the measure, which was imperatively demanded by the profession and the country. Mr. Blake, no doubt, rendered valuable aid to Mr. Baldwin in the framing of the bill, which was, nevertheless, introduced on the responsibility of the Government, and Mr. Baldwin especially, and I know that it was at Mr. Baldwin's earnest and pressing solicitations that Mr. Blake, at the very commencement of what promised to be a most brilliant political and professional career, consented to abandon it, in order to take a post, which no other man in the profession could have filled with so much advantage to the public. I have been glad of the opportunity of stating that up to the time of my leaving Canada in 1855, no political alliance was formed on the principle of securing majorities from the two Provinces. It was, of course, considered desirable that the Government should have a majority from each section in support of its policy. At the time of the crisis in 1842 there was every reason to believe that the Ministerial party was the strongest in the House, and it certainly could only have been defeated by a coalition between the Conservatives, led by Sir Allan Macnab, and the opposing Liberals led by Messrs. Lafontaine and Baldwin. Such a coalition would have resembled very much that between Fox and Lord North, but neither Mr. Lafontaine nor Mr. Baldwin would have consented to take office with Sir Allan Macnab. The new coalition was one between men who held common views of public policy, and it was completely successful, having been approved by all but an unanimous vote in the House. It is a circumstance not unworthy of notice that the Governor, who alone of all Lord Elgin's predecessors, is held in grateful remembrance by the French Canadian population, was a Conservative in his politics. Lords Durham, Sydenham and Metcalfe, though, all but especially the two first-named, decidedly Liberal, will never be so considered by French Canadians; while Sir Charles Bagot, I am inclined to think, stands at least as high as any other Governor in their estimation. Unfortunately that most upright and conscientious statesman was prostrated by sickness shortly after the reconstruction of the Administration, and was succeeded by Sir Charles, afterwards Lord Metcalfe. The choice of an Indian statesman of reputed ability, but without any experience whatever of Parliamentary government, was at least singular. It was well known at the time that the Secretary of State for the Colonies, the late Earl of Derby, disapproved of Sir Charles Bagot's policy, and there can now be little doubt that he formed a determination to overthrow Responsible Government, and selected Sir Charles Metcalfe as the most fitting agent for the purpose. If, as Mr. Withrow declares in his history, Lord Stanley had really adopted the policy of his predecessors, the Government of Canada presented no extraordinary difficulty at the time of Sir Charles Bagot's illness. The new Ministry had the largest Parliamentary support of any that has ever held office in Canada. The circumstances of Lord Metcalfe's appointment, with the light thrown on them by subsequent events, are calculated to excite grave suspicion that there was a foregone conclusion to overthrow Responsible Government. In Lord Metcalfe's life, the private note first addressed to him by Lord Stanley is published. His Lordship writes on the 14th January, 1843, enquiring as to Sir Charles Metcalfe's health, and asking him whether he would be able, and if able, disposed to take upon himself " most honorable, but at the " same time very arduous duties in the public service." In case of his consenting to undertake those duties he is requested to call at the Colonial Office, " where I should be happy to enter upon " an unreserved communication with you upon the subject." Of course, there is no information given as to the unreserved communication which was made when Sir Charles Metcalfe expressed his willingness to undertake the " arduous duties," but Sir Charles wrote to Captain Higginson, afterwards his Secretary:—

" I am not sure that the Government of Canada is a manageable affair, and unless I think I can go to a good purpose I will not go at all."

Such language is inexplicable on any other assumption than that the arduous duty was to overthrow Responsible Government. All Sir Charles Metcalfe's correspondence prior to his departure from England is indicative of a feeling that he was going on a "forlorn hope" expedition, and I feel assured that poor Sir Charles Bagot had a foreboding of what was likely to happen when in his last sad interview with his Ministers he more than once appealed to them "to defend his memory." It must be admitted that Lord Stanley could hardly have made choice of a man better suited for his purpose. Sir Charles Metcalfe's biographer describes him as "a statesman known to be saturated through and through with Liberal opinions," and such was the estimation in which he was held in England. In India, where his reputation had been acquired, or as Governor of a Crown Colony, he would have succeeded admirably, but a more unfit man to administer a constitutional Government on Lord Durham's principles could not have been selected. Sir Charles Metcalfe himself wrote to his sister:—

"Never was man dragged into public employment more against his will."

Again, to his friend Mr. Mangles, he wrote:—

"I never undertook anything with so much reluctance or so little hope of doing good. I fear that the little reputation that I have acquired is more likely to be damaged than improved in the troubled waters of Canada. If I succeed in reconciling local dissensions, I shall rejoice in having undertaken the charge; if I fail, which from the state of things is more probable, I must console myself with the assurance that for the rest of my days I shall be left undisturbed in the retirement that I love."

I shall dwell as briefly as possible on the Metcalfe crisis. It seems to me important to establish, 1st. The repugnance entertained by Lord Metcalfe to Responsible Government. 2nd. His almost inconceivable ignorance of the views of Lords Durham and Sydenham, and 3rd. The improper means taken to obtain a Parliamentary majority. In less than a month after his assumption of the Government Sir Charles Metcalfe declared in a despatch:—

"I find myself condemned, as it were, to carry on the Government to the utter exclusion of those on whom the mother country might confidently rely in the hour of need."

A month later he writes :—

"Now comes the tug of war, and supposing absolute submission to be out of the question I cannot say that I see the end of the struggle if the parties alluded to (the Council) really mean to maintain it."

Lord Metcalfe's biographer is very frank in his exposition of his Lordship's views. The declarations are so numerous that being unable to quote at much length I have found it difficult to select. I shall take one at random :—

"He was called upon to govern or to submit to the Government of Canada by a party, and the party by which he was to govern was one with which he had no sympathy. It was rather a combination of parties than a single faction—a combination of two parties—the principles of neither of which Metcalfe could bring himself to approve. He had some conception of the state of parties in the Province before he set his foot on Canadian soil, but he had no clear knowledge of the extent to which party spirit was eating into the very life of the colony or the embarrassment which must beset him as soon as ever he attempted to do justice to all classes and conditions of men irrespective of the factions to which they belonged."

I might cite many other passages to establish the fact of Sir Charles Metcalfe's opposition to Responsible Government as understood by the Canadian people and as established by the resolutions of 1841. In the extract that I have cited, there is no reference to Canadian public opinion as expressed by the Representatives of the people, but, on the contrary, it is manifest that the personal predilections of the Governor were to be the rule of his Government. I proceed to consider, 2ndly, the ignorance displayed by Sir Charles Metcalfe of the views of his predecessors on the subject of Responsible Government. In a remarkable despatch, dated 5th May, 1843, nearly four months before the resignation of his Ministers, he discussed the whole question. Regarding, he observes "Lord Sydenham as the fabricator of the frame of Government existing in this Province," he has carefully examined his despatches to ascertain "the precise view" which he took of Responsible Government. He infers from his earlier despatches that Lord Sydenham was wholly opposed to Responsible Government, and I am bound to admit that Lord Sydenham appears to have modified his views very considerably during his residence in Canada. His views, however, can only be ascertained from his acts. Sir Charles Metcalfe, professing to believe that Lord Sydenham was opposed to Responsible Government, observes:—

"It is beyond measure surprising that he adopted the very form of administration that was most assuredly calculated to defeat that purpose, and to produce or confirm the notion of Responsible Government, which he had before reprobated—that is the responsibility of Executive officers of the Government to the popular Legislative Assembly. In composing his Council of the principal Executive officers under his authority, requiring that they should all be members of the Legislature and chiefly of the popular branch, and in making their tenure of office dependent on their commanding a majority in the body representing the people, he seems to me to have ensured with the certainty of cause and effect that the Council of the Governor should regard themselves as responsible, not so much to the Governor as to the House of Assembly. In adopting the very form and practice of the Home Government, by which the principal Ministers of the Crown form a cabinet acknowledged by the nation as the Executive Administration and themselves acknowledging responsibility to Parliament, he rendered it inevitable that the Council here should obtain and ascribe to themselves, in at least some degree, the character of a Cabinet of Ministers. If Lord Sydenham did not intend this, he was more mistaken than from his known ability one would suppose to be possible,—and if he did intend it, he, with his eyes open, carried into practice that very theory of Responsible Colonial Government which he had pronounced his opinion decidedly against. I cannot presume to account for this apparent inconsistency otherwise than by supposing either that he had altered his opinion when he formed his Council after the union of the two Provinces, or that he yielded against his own conviction to some necessity which he found himself unable to resist."

It is quite immaterial whether Lord Sydenham yielded to conviction or to the force of circumstances; but no one can read the foregoing extract without acknowledging that in the controversy which Sir Charles Metcalfe subsequently raised with his Ministers, he could hardly have doubted that they were acting in accordance with the principle of government which he himself admitted had been fully established. It will always be a matter of uncertainty whether Lord Sydenham really yielded his opinions to circumstances or whether he purposely concealed them in order not to shock the prejudices which the Conservative party

entertained against Responsible Government. It was hardly possible, in view of the state of public opinion in Lower Canada, that the Governor who brought about the Union could enjoy the confidence of the French Canadians. Lord Sydenham was too experienced a statesman to have had any doubt as to the necessity of establishing Parliamentary Government, but the necessities of his position rendered it impossible for him to obtain the coöperation of those friendly to that system. I have already described the parties on whose support he determined to lean, and many of these were no friends to Responsible Government. Moreover, the system was new to the Canadians, and Lord Sydenham, who had himself been a Cabinet Minister, was but too ready to render all the aid in his power to the Ministers whose chief reliance was on his personal influence. In a subsequent part of the despatch from which I have last quoted, Sir Charles Metcalfe displays an ignorance that is simply amazing. He asserts that "the term Respon-
" sible Government now in general use in this colony was derived,
" I am told, from marginal notes of Lord Durham's report."
Prior to that the Democratic party " had no precise name for the
" object of their desires, and could not exactly define their views."
Can it be conceived possible that Sir Charles Metcalfe was ignorant of the great contest for Responsible Government during Sir Francis Head's administration in 1836, or that the term was clearly understood by the Canadian statesmen both of 'Lower and Upper Canada long before that time? The motto of the Toronto *Examiner* during the whole period of Lord Durham's Government was " Responsible Government," and the precise recommendations of his Lordship's report regarding that principle of Government were perseveringly advocated in the columns of that journal from its commencement in July, 1838—as a reference to its files would prove. But not satisfied with asserting that Canadian Reformers did not understand what they were contending for, Sir Charles Metcalfe expressed an opinion that Lord Durham himself had no intention of conceding what it was the special object of his report to recommend. He seized on the following expression, which he himself failed to comprehend, as justifying his opinion :—I find that he proposes that all officers of the Government, " except the
" Governor and his Secretary, should be responsible to the united
" Legislature, and that the Governor should carry on his Govern-
" ment by heads of departments in whom the United Legislature

" repose confidence." On which Sir Charles sagaciously remarks:

"If the Secretary who issued the Governor's orders were not responsible to the Legislature, there would be a great difference from the present arrangement under which the Provincial administration generally is carried on through Secretaries professedly so responsible."

In the extracts which I have cited from Lord Durham's report there is no room for misconception, and I would especially refer to the recommendation that "the official acts of the Governor should be countersigned by some public functionary," so as to insure responsibility. It is hardly necessary to point out the difference between his (the Governor's) Secretary and the Secretary of the Province. The Governors have always had the assistance of Secretaries, who of course are in no sense responsible to Parliament. I shall now advert to the third point on which history must condemn Lord Metcalfe, viz., the improper means which he adopted to obtain a majority in Parliament. No one can read the biography of Lord Metcalfe and his numerous despatches without being thoroughly convinced of his hostility to Responsible Government, and yet for months after his rupture with his Ministers he spared no efforts to persuade the people of Canada that he was a sincere friend to that principle, and that but for the unconstitutional demands of his Ministers he would have gone on with them cordially. Among those whom he completely deceived was a venerable French-Canadian statesman, Hon. D. B. Viger, whose pamphlets afford unmistakeable evidence that he labored under a misapprehension as to the cause of the rupture. If Mr. Viger could have read the despatches of Sir Charles Metcalfe to the Secretary of State prior to the resignation of the Ministers, I am fully persuaded that he would never have accepted office. I look back with feelings of pride and satisfaction to the circumstances under which I first took up my residence in Montreal about the close of the year 1843. I had previously been connected with the press, and had endeavored to be the exponent of the views of the Reformers of Upper Canada, but after the crisis of 1843, it was deemed most desirable, in the interests of the United Liberal party, that there should be a journal at the seat of Government in the confidence of the political leaders of both sections, and I was strongly urged to establish such a journal, and I readily undertook the work, although fully aware of the fearful responsibility which I incurred at a period when party politicians had to endure an amount of odium of which those of the present day have only a faint idea. When I commenced my career as a journalist in Montreal early in 1844, an election for the city was pending, the candidates being Mr., afterwards Judge, Drummond, and the late Mr. William Molson, a gentleman for whom personally I entertained as high a respect as any of his supporters could have done. A great principle was at stake, and I laboured with all the zeal in my power for the popular candidate, who was eventually returned by a majority of 920. It is stated by Sir Charles Metcalfe, in his despatch of 23rd November, 1844, that—

"The British party seemed determined to win the election, (referring to the general election), or, at least, not to have their suffrages taken from them by the violence practised at Mr. Drummond's election in April. The same violence was designed by that gentleman and his party on this occasion, but the British party were resolved to oppose force by force, and organized themselves for defence. Owing to the spirit and firmness with which they resisted the attacks of the Roman Catholic mobs of canal laborers hired by Mr. Drummond's party—to the admirable arrangement of the returning officers which secured uninterrupted and equal polling for both sides throughout the election, and to the ready attendance of the military when necessary to preserve the peace, the violence attempted entirely failed and the British party triumphed."

The foregoing passage would lead to the inference that a peaceable majority had been in danger of being deprived of their rights owing to the violent proceedings of Roman Catholic mobs of canal laborers not possessed of the franchise. But strange to say, Sir Charles Metcalfe in his very next sentence proceeds to destroy his own case.

"As it is supposed (he proceeds) that if all the electors could have voted there would have been a majority in favor of the Opposition candidates, owing to the great bulk of the French-Canadian and Irish Roman Catholic voters being on their side, the peculiar circumstances which gave success to the British party require explanation. The existing election law, confining the polling to two days, does not allow time for receiving all the votes of so large a constituency. The polling, therefore, being carried on equally in those wards in which neither party's votes were exhausted, there was a majority in favor of the candidates supporting Her Majesty's Government, which secured their success without ascertaining on which side the majority of the aggregate body of electors actually was, as the whole, for want of time, could not be brought to the polls. In the April election, the polls having been seized by the hired ruffians of Mr. Drummond, and the British party being unable to resist from want of organization, the returning officers also either being partial or devoid of energy and firmness, the British party had then no chance. On the present occasion the numbers were, for Mr. Moffat 1079, Mr. De Bleury 1075, for Mr. Drummond 953, Dr. Beaubien 952."

Such is Sir Charles Metcalfe's own account of this memorable election. I shall give you that of the *Pilot* :—

" The city is divided into six wards, three of which are so small that in three hours all the votes they contain can be polled. In two of these three, it is well known that the Tories have always had an aggregate majority of about 100. In the three other wards, which contain five-sixths of the votes of the city, the Liberals could command in one 3 to 1, and in the other two 4 to 1. Now, it will be observed that by means of the alternate voting, without the consent of the Liberal candidates, it was utterly impossible to record in two days even one-half of the votes of the great wards, and hence it was that the Liberals of the city have been as effectually disfranchised under the paternal despotism of Sir Charles Metcalfe, as they were under the honest tyranny of a Sydenham, a tyranny which Sir Charles Metcalfe, on his arrival in this country, professed to condemn."

You will not have failed to notice that Sir Charles Metcalfe himself admitted that " the bulk of the French Canadian and " Irish Roman Catholic votes were in favor of the Opposition " candidate," indeed he commenced his account of the election by remarking, " the carrying of the Montreal election in favor of the " Government was hardly expected." The means resorted to are stated with great frankness, except that there was an omission to mention that all the oaths were put by the agents of the Government candidates to all the voters, old men being sworn to their being of the age of 21, for the purpose of delay. The Opposition candidates maintained that voting by tallies could only be admitted when both parties gave their consent, and that it was beyond the power of the returning officer to direct the observance of such a practice. The disfranchisement of the Suburbs by Lord Sydenham was an admission that the majority was on the Opposition

side, and the election of Mr. Drummond a few months previously
by a majority of 920, obtained entirely in the Suburb Wards,
could have left no room for doubt as to which party commanded
the majority of votes. It may likewise be observed that at the
next election Messrs. Lafontaine and Holmes were returned by a
majority of 1,300. Some recent references to those old times
have partly induced me to place on record a true statement of the
successive disfranchisements of the City of Montreal upwards of
30 years ago. Violence at elections has long since entirely
ceased, but historical truth and justice render it proper to establish the fact that the great majority of the electors of Montreal
were unflinching in their oposition to the reactionary policy of Sir
Charles Metcalfe, which, nevertheless, had a temporary success.
During about four years of opposition the united Liberal party waited patiently for another appeal to the constituencies of the country.
The Government majority was small, and obtained entirely from
Upper Canada, the Opposition having a considerable majority in
Lower Canada. Lord Metcalfe, who had suffered during the
whole period of his government from a painful disease, was at
length compelled to resign in November, 1845, his Government
having lasted less than three years. He received an assurance
from Lord Stanley that "your administration of affairs in Canada
" has more than realized the most sanguine expectations which I
" had ventured to form of it," an assurance strongly confirmatory
of what I have already said of His Lordship's object in selecting
Sir Charles Metcalfe having been to overthrow Responsible Government. Earl Cathcart, the Commander of the Forces, succeeded to the Government, and during his short administration
made no change. In 1846 there was a change of Government in
England, and Earl Grey succeeded Lord Stanley at the Colonial
Office, and, shortly after his assumption of office, selected the Earl
of Elgin as Governor General of Canada. From the period of his
arrival Lord Elgin manifested a fixed determination not to be embroiled in the personal controversies of his predecessors. Government House became once more neutral ground, where no party distinctions were recognized. The general election which took place
about the close of the year 1847 resulted in the complete triumph
of the Liberal party, and the consequent return of their leaders
to power on the meeting of Parliament in February, 1848. This
seems a convenient place to refer to the composition of the rival

parties. Lord Metcalfe invariably, in his despatches, divided the population into French-Canadians, Reformers and Conservatives, as if the French-Canadians took no interest in the political questions which divided parties, but were seeking some special objects of their own. It is, I think, a more correct definition to describe the Reform party as consisting of the bulk of the French-Canadians, of the Irish Roman Catholics, and a small Protestant minority in Lower Canada, and a majority of the Protestant denominations other than the Church of England in Upper Canada, to which may be added the Irish Roman Catholics of that Province. There was greater division among the Presbyterians and Methodists than among the other denominations, especially during the political crises of 1836 and 1843-44. The great majority of the members of the Church of England, and many Presbyterians and Methodists constituted the Conservative party in Upper Canada, while in Lower Canada the great majority of the population of English and Scotch origin, and of the Irish Protestants were members of the same party. The administration which came into office in 1848 had to encounter a most violent opposition from the Conservatives on their bill for granting compensation to the sufferers from the wanton destruction of property during the rebellions of 1837-38. The excitement was general, but unfortunately, owing to the City of Montreal having been the seat of Government, the manifestations of displeasure were more pronounced in this city, where the buildings in which the meetings of the Legislature were temporarily held, although the property of the city, were destroyed by some of the irritated citizens in a moment of frenzy, and such further violence displayed as to enable those who had always been unfriendly to Montreal to succeed in effecting the removal of the Government from that city. It is to be noted that the violent proceedings of the opposition in 1849 had the effect of strengthening the Ministers with their supporters in both sections of the Province. Even those who did not fully approve of the Rebellion Losses bill comprehended the objection to an appeal to England to disallow an act deliberately concurred in by the Canadian Parliament. The discontented party published a manifesto in favor of annexation to the United States, but it met with little response from the Conservatives of Upper Canada, and was really a mere exhibition of the irritation which prevailed very extensively among the

British population of Lower Canada, and for which great allowance should be made by an impartial narrator of the history of the period. In 1850 the Legislature met in Toronto, and by that time there had been premonitory symptoms of a rupture in the Liberal party. It cannot be expected that there will be the same unanimity among the members of a party of progress as in one formed to resist organic changes. In the former there will always be a section dissatisfied with what they think the inertness of their leaders. I have to explain as clearly as in my power the principles and views of those who, though elected as Reformers, ceased to extend support to Mr. Lafontaine's administration, and gradually assumed a still more hostile attitude, and combined with the Conservative Opposition to overthrow the Government, which succeeded it. This new Opposition, if I may so term it, was composed of members from Lower Canada, chiefly French-Canadians, and members from Upper Canada, but between these sections there was no similarity of views, as I shall be able to show. The founder of the Opposition party in Lower Canada was the celebrated Louis Joseph Papineau, who, on re-entering Parliament in 1848, placed himself in open and decided opposition to the Government, and to nearly all his countrymen then having seats in the Legislature. I cannot refer to so distinguished a man as Mr. Papineau without pausing to state the impression which I formed of him during the brief period of our intercourse. I had never seen him prior to his return from France, whither he had retreated after the rebellion of 1837. It was impossible to avoid being charmed by his conversation and demeanour in private life, but his political principles were moulded by circumstances, which seemed to render him incapable of appreciating the conduct of those, on whom the leadership of his countrymen had devolved in his absence. I am convinced that his guiding principle was an utter distrust of all English statesmen. He knew that the avowed object of the Union had been to destroy the influence of his countrymen, and he never would consent to give it a trial. Moreover, he was, after his return to Canada, and possibly at an earlier period of his life, a confirmed Republican, and never could place the slightest confidence in Responsible Government, as a means of securing local independence. He had no Parliamentary success during the few years that he remained in public life on his return to Canada, but he was the founder of the Lower Canada Liberal Opposition, which became more formidable under the leadership of younger men. In a lecture delivered a few months ago, by the Hon. Mr. Laurier, M.P., reference is made to the history of this party, and it has been satisfactory to me to have had an opportunity of reading the account given of it by one, who has derived his information of the events of that period by other means than personal observation. In a great deal of the introductory portion of Mr. Laurier's lecture, I myself entirely concur, but in eulogizing Liberalism it must never be forgotten that it is a relative term. Mr. Laurier has quoted largely from the writings of Lord Macaulay, who was a special favourite of my own, but in almost the last speech made in the House of Commons by that eminent man in 1853, he used these words:—"For myself, sir, I hope that I am at once a Liberal and a Conservative politician." I can draw no other inference from Mr. Laurier's own language, than that had he been in public life at the time, he would have been, as I was, a Conservative in opposition to the Liberalism of *L'Avenir*. There is, it appears to me, a fundamental error in Mr. Laurier's history of the Liberal party. He pronounces an eulogium on both Mr. Lafontaine and Mr. Papineau as "men who loved their country ardently, passionately, who devoted their lives to it, who were disinterested and upright," and so far I entirely concur with him, but when he proceeds to declare further that he "will not undertake to criticize the respective political views of those great men," and when he recommends his hearers not to enquire which of the two was right and which was wrong, it seems to me that he has wholly failed in a most important part of the task which he undertook. It was obviously the duty of an impartial historian, and one from which Mr. Laurier's favorite Lord Macaulay would not have shrunk, to have defined as precisely as possible the grounds on which Mr. Papineau and his followers deemed it proper to create a division in the Liberal party. Mr. Laurier, it is true, has been less reticent on the subject of the disciples of Mr. Papineau, those who "after supporting Mr. Lafontaine in the glorious struggle with Lord Metcalfe, abandoned him for the more advanced policy of Mr. Papineau." He states that these founders of the Liberal party, emboldened by success, founded *L'Avenir*, and issued a programme of not less than 21 articles, which commenced with the election of magistrates and ended with annexation to the United States. In condemning those views Mr. Laurier excuses those who hold them, on account of their youth, although they were clearly imbibed from the veteran politician Mr. Papineau. Another excuse is even less valid. It is not fair to assert that in 1848 the new constitution had not been applied in good faith by the Colonial Office. Not only had all the utterances of the Earl of Elgin been most satisfactory, but the presence of Mr. Lafontaine and of his colleagues in the Cabinet ought to have been held as a sufficient guarantee that Responsible Government was fully established. Great stress is laid by Mr. Laurier on the services rendered by *L'Avenir* party towards the abolition of the seigniorial tenure. This is, in my judgment, one of the questions on which an immense amount of misconception exists, but it would be wholly impossible for me to discuss it on such an occasion as the present, and I will merely state that *L'Avenir* party sought the reduction of the *cens et rentes* without compensation to the seigniors, and that the bill introduced by the Government in 1854, though coming very far short of the demands of that party, was, nevertheless, so objectionable that it was completely remodelled in the Legislative Council, and the money voted by Parliament applied to the abolition of the casual rights, which were the real public grievance, and not to the extinction or reduction of the *cens et rentes*. I emphatically deny that the party of *L'Avenir* are entitled to the credit accorded to them by Mr. Laurier, in connection with the settlement of the Seigniorial question.

[Having taken considerable interest in the settlement of the seigniorial question in 1854, and having, while the bill passed by the Legislative Assembly was under the consideration of the Legislative Council, published a *brochure* entitled "The Seigniorial Tenure—Present state of the Question; by a member of the Legislative Assembly of Upper Canada," I shall endeavor to give the substance of that long-forgotten paper. It commenced by noticing the bill which emanated from the Select Committee of 1851, which proposed to define by law the maximum amount of *cens et rentes* to which the seignior should be entitled, and to compel him to concede his unoccupied lands at that rate. This bill, which was in the nature of a declaratory bill, was opposed by Mr. Lafontaine, who pronounced it a measure of confiscation. It was reported from the committee so late in the session that legislative action on the subject before the prorogation became impossible. Mr. Lafontaine's retirement from public life took place during the recess, and after the formation of a new government a general election took place. During the session of 1852-3 a bill was introduced which proposed to reduce what were held to be exorbitant rents, and to obtain from the courts of justice a decision as to the legality of such rents, to compensate the seigniors in case they were legal for any excess over 2d per acre, which was in future to be the maximum rent; if illegal, the seignior was to submit to the reduction without compensation. It is unnecessary to enter upon other details, as the burthen of the commutation of the casual rights was to fall on the *censitaires*. The bill as passed by the Assembly was rejected by the Legislative Council. The next bill, submitted in 1854, was based on a reduction of the *cens et rentes* to 1d per acre, the professed object being to meet the demands of the district of Quebec, where the rents were much lower than in Montreal. But while the bill was in committee, the principle of compulsory commutation of the casual rights was introduced, and in a manner, as I contended, which would be unjust to the seigniors; while on the other hand any forced commutation that would have done justice to the seigniors would have been most repugnant to the *censitaires*. It was pointed out that the great objection to all the schemes that had been proposed was their unequal operation, both as regarded the seigniors and the *censitaires*, while the liberal indemnity fund would be wasted. It was urged that inasmuch as it had at last been admitted that the tenure should be abolished, the wisest policy would be to apply the indemnity to the extinction of the most onerous and at the same time the most odious of the rights, the legality of which was nevertheless undisputed. After pointing out that even the *censitaires* who were subject to what were held to be exorbitant rents would have no just cause of complaint, it concluded by stating that the advantage of the proposed plan was that no one would have to pay more annual rent than he actually paid, while all society would be relieved of the feudal burthens. The views which I contended for were substantially those adopted by the Legislative Council, by which body the bill sent from the Assembly was completely changed, and I had reason to believe at the time that my little *brochure* had been useful. The popular feeling repre sented by the party of *L'Avenir* was entirely directed to the reduction of the rents, and not to the abolition of the tenure; and while I admit that the rents were what pressed most on the masses of the people, they were by no means objectionable on public grounds like many of the casual rights, such, especially, as the *lods et ventes* and the *droit de retrait*, which was often most unfairly exercised.]

In 1852 the Opposition published a new journal, called *Le Pays*, and it would be interesting to know whether this change of front was caused by pressure from their allies in Upper Canada, who most assuredly had no sympathy with the views enunciated in the programme of *L'Avenir*. It is certainly most extraordinary that Mr. Laurier should have undertaken to give the history of the Liberal party in Lower Canada alone, although it was, from the time of its formation, necessarily forced to act in Parliament with men of another origin, and with widely different views on many points. As I may not find it convenient to refer again to Mr. Laurier's lecture, I may observe here that his statement that the section of the Liberal party which followed Mr. Lafontaine "finit apres quelques tatonnements par s'allier aux Tories du "Haut Canada," is quite incorrect. There were no "tatonnements," and the Lower Canada Government party had a considerable majority, of which, had Mr. Laurier been then in Parliament, and had he held the views expressed in his lecture, he would have formed part. A section of the liberal party, including those who had adopted the programme of *L'Avenir*, and the Upper Canada Reformers, who had withdrawn their confidence from the Government on other grounds, united with the Conservative opposition to defeat the Ministry. Whether they were justified in doing so, is not now the question. They acted on their responsibility; but the effect of their proceeding was to force the alliance, or coalition, which Mr. Laurier condemns. The Government must be carried on, and all combinations must give way to that supreme necessity. The Ministry having been forced to resign, the leader of the Opposition was sent for, according to usage, and when it appeared, after conferences, that there were no essential points of difference between the two parties, they united to carry on the Government. My complaint against Mr. Laurier is, that he has represented a proceeding which arose from inevitable necessity, as one of premeditation.

THE CLEAR GRIT DEPARTURE.

I must now advert to the policy of the Opposition in Upper Canada. It would be wholly out of my power, on such an occasion as the present, to do more than glance very briefly at the questions on which a portion of the Upper Canada Liberals took a different view from the members of the Government. Some of those questions chiefly affected Upper, others Lower Canada. The former were the clergy reserves, rectory and sectarian school questions; the latter, grants to charitable corporations, connected with the Catholic Church, and Acts creating what were termed ecclesiastical corporations. On some of these questions wide differences of opinion prevailed between the bulk of the supporters of the Government in Lower Canada and a considerable number of their supporters in Upper Canada. All these questions, most fortunately, have been removed from the field of politics; but they were at one time very exciting, and had a most important influence in causing the disruption of the old Reform party. Complaints of the inertness of the Government on the clergy reserve question, which was the most prominent of those engaging public attention in Upper Canada, were assiduously made during 1850, although a member of the Government proposed and carried an address to the Crown praying for a repeal of the Imperial Clergy Reserve Act, so that the whole question might be settled in accordance with Canadian public opinion. I desire, as much as possible, to avoid a recurrence to past controversies, and to explain the causes of the rupture of the Liberal party without discussing the merits of the respective views of the opposing sections. I can hardly do this better than by making a quotation or two from the writings of the Hon. George Brown, then conducting the *Globe* newspaper, which was the chief organ of the Liberal Opposition.

THE BROAD PROTESTANT CRY.

Shortly before the general election of 1851, Mr. Brown addressed a series of letters to me as the Leader of the Government, from which I select the following passage:—

"You know that I have been at open issue with you throughout in regard to your systematic disregard of the feelings and wishes of your supporters, and the disastrous effects on the party thereby produced. You know that the *Globe's* resistance of

Roman Catholic aggression caused the first open rupture between us."

Unfortunately, I complained of the "systematic disregard of the feelings and wishes" of our allies in Lower Canada of the Roman Catholic faith, on the part of the *Globe* and those of the Reform party who supported its views. I never could be convinced that there was any tendency whatever towards aggression on the part of Roman Catholics. I did not consider that the claims on the part of the Roman Catholics to have separate schools in Upper Canada, as the Protestants had always had in Lower Canada, or the claim to have educational or charitable institutions incorporated with a right to hold property, were acts of aggression. I considered, moreover, that, irrespective of the special merits of the questions at issue, great respect should be paid to the wishes of the great majority of the population of Lower Canada, with whom the Liberals of Upper Canada were in cordial alliance, and on whose support they depended for procuring the settlement of questions in which they took an interest. In the same number of the *Globe*, from which I have quoted, in reply to an article in a Ministerial Liberal paper, expressing a belief that on certain questions, "Clergy Reserves, and one or two others," on which the French members entertained prejudices, they would be guided by the results of the next elections. It is said:—

"Will the *American* dare say that 'a large number of the leading men' among the French members have declared their willingness to be guided by the results of the next elections on the Rectory question? or on the Sectarian School question? or on the Sectarian moneygrant question? or on the marriage question? We believe there is some truth in the statement as regards the clergy reserves, but in regard to any other there is none whatever."

It is with no intention of impeaching the accuracy of the foregoing statement that I have cited it, but to establish the cause of the disruption of the Reform party, owing to irreconcilable differences of opinion on important questions between a large section of that party in Upper Canada and the Government supported by the bulk of the Liberal party in Lower Canada, and, if the members elected were to be considered as a guide, by the majority of the Reformers in Upper Canada. I must confess that I was less surprised than disappointed at the divergence of views to which I have just called your attention among those who had long formed an united Liberal party in the old Province of Upper Canada. For a period of ten years the absorbing political question on which the parties had been divided was the establishment of Responsible or Parliamentary Government, and it must be obvious that persons differing widely on other questions might concur in advocating a measure calculated to benefit the community at large. The questions next in importance were those known as the Clergy Reserve and University questions, and as the object of the Reformers was to wrest public endowments of lands from the Church of England for the common benefit of all classes of the population, there was no difficulty in securing a concurrence of action between the Roman Catholics and those Protestants who were opposed to the claims of the Church of England. When, however, other questions engaged public consideration, it soon became apparent that there were differences of opinion between the sections of the Liberal party to which I have referred, which rendered harmonious action between them impossible. The population of Upper Canada was composed largely of immigrants from the United Kingdom, who brought with them the animosities which they had inherited from their ancestors, and which originated in causes with which all acquainted with the past history of the Mother Country are acquainted. Cordial co-operation between Roman Catholics and Evangelical Protestants can scarcely be expected when questions are at issue involving scruples of conscience on the part of either, and there is perhaps more cause for wonder that the alliance lasted for more than ten years than that it was at length dissolved.

PARTY CONVENTIONS.

About the time that Mr. Brown's letters were published, a convention of delegates was held in the County of Oxford, which I then represented and for which I intended to be a candidate at the approaching election, the object of which was to require their candidate to pledge himself to support the principles maintained by the section of the party in opposition to the Government, which was led by Mr. Brown. I was accordingly applied to by letter and informed of the condition on which I had been selected as the nominee of the Convention. The correspondence, in view of subsequent events, may not be thought out of place as bearing on the history of parties:

HONORABLE SIR,—You will see by the resolutions adopted on the 15th instant, that I am requested to send you a copy and request your assent to the same. I therefore trust that you will forward the same at your earliest convenience.

I remain yours truly,
THOMAS HARDY.

QUEBEC, 29th Oct., 1851.

SIR,—I have the honor to acknowledge the receipt of your letter, without date, enclosing "copy of a political platform resolved upon by the Convention, in convention assembled, in Woodstock, on Thursday, October 15, 1851;" and also a copy of certain resolutions adopted by the same convention, one of which is to the effect "that the Hon. Francis Hincks, the nominee of this Convention, be instructed and required by the Chairman of this Convention to subscribe to the platform of the reform party in the County of Oxford, as expressed in convention this day," while by another I am required, as the nominee of the said Convention, to resign my seat in parliament when called upon by two-thirds of the said Convention. I shall, I trust, be excused by the gentlemen composing the Convention referred to if I reply to your communication at some length, and if I address you with perfect frankness and sincerity, even though my views should be found unpalatable by those to whom I desire to have hem submitted, and for whom individually and collectively I entertain a high respect. You will permit me to say, that I cannot recognize any right in a convention of delegates, appointed in a way unknown to the Constitution, to impose conditions of any kind upon candidates for the suffrages of the freeholders of the county. The course taken by certain conventions in the western part of Upper Canada has already, I am grieved to find, enabled the opponents of progressive reform to charge them with attempting, like the socialist clubs of France, to exercise an unconstitutional control over the government and parliament of the country. It is, I am sure, far from the intention of any of the gentlemen with whom you are associated, to be a party to proceedings which might be fairly so characterized, and I therefore feel great confidence that, on mature consideration, the delegates to the County of Oxford Convention will give me their support without conditions which it would be equally degrading for them to impose and for me to submit to. As an executive councillor I am bound by my oath of office to advise the representative of our Sovereign to adopt that policy which I believe to be the best. In giving that advice conscientiously, I must be guided by the circumstances in which the entire Province is placed, and by the general state of public opinion. If circumstances and the state of public opinion be such that it is inexpedient to carry out the policy which I deem most conducive to the common weal, my duty is to retire from office, so as to enable others to carry on the government. Were I to enter office fettered by pledges to a convention having no constitutional responsibility, it would be obviously impossible for me either to act in concert with others or to give free advice to the representative of my Sovereign. I should, in fact, cease to be a minister of the Crown, responsible to parliament for my advice, and be the mere delegate of a convention elected in a manner wholly unknown to the Constitution. While I am bound frankly to assure you that nothing could induce me to occupy such a position as that which I have described, it is also my duty to inform you, that were I to subscribe to your conditions, I should have to abandon my seat in the Cabinet, and, with it, the prospect of advancing that cause which many of you have much at heart. With regard to my views on the great questions which have agitated the public mind, the Convention cannot be in ignorance, as I had an opportunity of addressing them very recently in public, as well as of explaining myself to most of them individually. Since then a new Administration has been formed, which will, I trust, receive in my person the support of a majority of the freeholders of the county of Oxford. I have already warned those persons who hold extreme views—some of them, in my opinion, inconsistent with our present Constitution, if not with British connection— that by pressing those views against the public opinion of other parts of the Province, they will endanger the success of measures of vital importance to the country, and secure the triumph of their opponents. My warnings may be disregarded, and the Reform party may, notwithstanding my efforts to prevent it, go disunited to the hustings. If so, I shall have the satisfaction of knowing that the responsibility will not rest with me. It is proper that I should here state my views with regard to the legitimate duties and powers of delegates elected in the manner generally adopted in Upper Canada. I can recognize the propriety of appointing delegates from the different sections of a county, for the purpose of effecting an amicable adjustment of the claims of rival candidates for the suffrages of the freeholders, which candidates entertain the same general views and appeal for support to the same party. It must be perfectly obvious that in my case no such convention was called for. In my position, as a member of the Government, all the supporters of that Government must be favorable to me; and it is my duty both to them, to myself, and to the entire party supporting the Government, to take the sense of the electors at the polls. The Convention in the county of Oxford was appointed by persons who, for reasons into which I need not enter, had modified their support to the Government as formerly constituted. The real question which, in my opinion, that Convention is called upon to decide, is, whether, under existing circumstances, it is expedient to divide the Reform party in the county of Oxford by setting up a candidate in opposition to me. This is what you and your friends must determine on your own responsibility; I may, however, be permitted to say that the course which I lately adopted, when called upon to advise the Governor-General with regard to the reconstruction of the Cabinet, was the constitutional mode of strengthening the Government in the opinion of those on whose support its existence depends. Should such tests as yours be applied to the Government candidates, the desired result will not be attained. To speak plainly, you may rely on it that if there be disunion among the Reformers of the county of Oxford, the example will be followed in other counties, to the serious injury of the entire party. I need not enlarge on this point. I shall appeal to the freeholders of the county of Oxford as a member of the present Government, and claiming for it this mark of confidence; and if the delegates of the Convention think proper to put up a candidate in opposition to me, I shall cheerfully bow to the decision given at the polls between that candidate and myself, and any other who may present himself. I have abstained in this reply from the discussion of the various questions submitted to me by the delegates—on some of which my opinions are known to be as liberal as those of any member of the Convention—because I feel that the true security for the public must be the characters of the responsible Ministers of the Crown, who have entire confidence in one another, and who feel that they can cordially cöoperate in effecting a settlement of all leading questions in a manner that will be satisfactory to the country.

I am, sir,
Your obedient servant,
F. HINCKS.

THOS. HARDY, Esq.

The Convention nominated a candidate, who was afterwards withdrawn, and I was elected.

THE HINCKS-MORIN GOVERNMENT.

It was shortly before this time that, in consequence of the retirement of Mr. Lafontaine from public life, I was sent for by the Earl of Elgin to advise him as to the construction of a new Government. Being well aware of the distrust that had been created as to my intentions on the subject of the Clergy Reserves, I was anxious to obtain the co-operation of some of those Reformers in whom the dissatisfied section of the party had professed to place implicit confidence. After some difficulties, all of a personal character, the new Administration was formed, and the result of the general election was to give it a fair working majority. One of the most urgent measures of reform was a bill for increasing the representation, which, although carried by a considerable majority during the administration of Mr. Lafontaine, had not obtained the consent of two-thirds of the Houses, as required by the Union Act. This bill was at last carried, and no effort was spared to procure the repeal of the Imperial Clergy Reserve Act. During a visit which I paid to England in 1852, I pressed this measure on the Secretary of State with all the energy in my power, but in vain. [I think it right, in justice as well to myself as to the memory of the Hon. Robert Baldwin, to disprove the following statement in Withrow's history, which I have reason to think is believed by many, as well as by the author named and some other contemporary writers.

"The discussion of the Clergy Reserve question was renewed outside of the House, principally in the journals of the advanced Reform party, the chief of which were the *Globe* and *Examiner* of Toronto. The older and more moderate Reformers, of whom Mr. Baldwin and Mr. Lafontaine may be regarded as types, *opposed the re-opening of this question, and sought to maintain the settlement of the subject* that had been effected by Parliament during Lord Sydenham's administration. Another section of the Reform party, which was rapidly rising into influence, wished for their entire secularisation. A division in the ranks of the party thus took place, which led to the retirement of some of its ablest members."

I have italicised the statements which I shall prove to be incorrect; but I may likewise affirm here that no question relating to the Clergy Reserves led to the retirement of any member of the Reform Administration. Between Mr. Baldwin and myself there was an entire concurrence of opinion on the question up to the period of his resignation in 1851; and I have no reason to doubt that he approved of the subsequent proceedings of the Government of which I was the leader. I have elsewhere mentioned Mr. Baldwin's entrance into public life about the year 1829,

He was a member of the Tenth Parliament of Upper Canada, which, in two consecutive sessions, passed bills, without a division, for the sale of the Clergy Reserves, and the application of the proceeds to educational purposes. Mr. Baldwin, although a most sincere member of the Church of England, was a strong advocate of religious equality; and although he had not, like the members of several denominations of Protestants, any conscientious objections to religious endowments, he was thoroughly convinced that they were indefensible in Canada. He was not in public life when the Clergy Reserve question was settled in 1840, by an Act of the Imperial Parliament, with which the Canadian Parliament could not constitutionally interfere, and he was well aware of the strong feeling that existed among the leaders of both political parties in England against Canadian legislation on that subject by the United Legislature. How strong that feeling was will appear from Sir John Pakington's despatch of December 1852. The first agitation on the subject after the passing of the Imperial Act proceeded from the friends of the Church of England. The Liberal Government had taken steps to have the Clergy Lands valued, with a view to their prompt sale; but in January, 1844, Governor-General Sir Charles Metcalfe proposed to the Secretary of State that the Clergy Reserve Lands should be vested in the religious bodies. Mr. Gladstone, then Secretary of State, pointed out that the Imperial Act would have to be amended, and asked for information. On the 6th April, 1846, the Executive Council recommended the suspension of all sales, and also the raising of the price of the lands valued by appraisers, from 25 to 125 per cent. In the next Session, Mr. Attorney-General Sherwood proposed an address to the Crown, praying Parliament to pass an Act authorizing a division of the lands, instead of the income arising from their proceeds, among the religious bodies. This was the signal for renewed agitation against the Imperial settlement. I was not a member of the Second Parliament of United Canada; but Mr. Baldwin and Mr. Price both spoke strongly against Mr. Sherwood's address, which was lost by 37 to 14. In 1849, the year of the rebellion losses bill, several petitions were presented against the existing settlement. In 1850, Mr. Price proposed a series of resolutions, on which to found an Address to the Crown for the repeal of the Clergy Reserve Act, for all of which Mr. Baldwin voted; and there can be no doubt that he would have voted for secularisation whenever the proper time came. That he was firmly convinced that no other settlement would be satisfactory, I can affirm in the most positive manner; and I trust that there will be no further assertions or insinuations to the contrary. Of course the policy adopted to effect the desired object is fairly open to criticism; and with regard to that, owing to his withdrawal from the Government in 1851, I have a greater load of responsibility than Mr. Baldwin, although there was entire concurrence between us in the incipient proceedings. Our plan was to obtain, firstly, the repeal of the Imperial Act, and then to legislate in accordance with Canadian public opinion.

Accordingly, during the Session of 1850, Mr. Price a member of the Administration, and one who, as a Congregationalist, had conscientious objections to religious endowments, was selected to move resolutions on which to found an address to the Crown for the repeal of the Imperial Clergy Reserve Act. The Address contains a narrative of the various attempts made during successive years to settle the question, all of which were frustrated by the action of the Legislative Council. It is unnecessary for me to quote more than the despatch of the Earl of Elgin to Earl Grey transmitting the address, the most important clause of which is embodied in it. That despatch, as will appear from Mr. Brown's letter was made the ground of suspicion against the administration:

Copy of a Despatch from the Right Hon. the EARL OF ELGIN *and* KINCARDINE *to the Right Hon. the* EARL GREY :

GOVERNMENT HOUSE, TORONTO, July 19, 1850.

MY LORD,—I have the honor to transmit herewith, in compliance with the request of the Legislative Assembly, to be laid at the foot of the Throne, an Address from that House to Her Majesty, on the subject of the Clergy Reserves. After recapitulating the proceedings of the House of Assembly of Upper Canada before the union of the Provinces in connexion with this question, it concludes with the prayer, that Her Majesty will be graciously pleased to recommend to Parliament a measure for the repeal of the Imperial Act 3 and 4 Vict., chap. 78, and for enabling the Canadian Parliament to dispose of the Clergy Reserves, subject to the condition of securing the stipends or allowances assigned from this fund to the clergy of the Churches of England or Scotland, or to any other religious bodies or denominations of Christians, to the parties now receiving them during their natural lives or incumbencies. It was finally carried by a majority of 46 votes to 23; some of the minority voting against it in consequence of this reservation.

2. It may be proper, however, to observe, that a much closer division took place on the passage of the 29th, in the series of resolutions on which the Address was founded, and which was thus worded:—" *Resolved*—That this House is of opinion, that when all the circumstances connected with this question are taken into consideration, no religious denomination can be held to have such vested interest in the revenue derived from the proceeds of the said Clergy Reserves as should prevent further legislation with reference to the disposal of them; but this House is nevertheless of opinion, that the claims of existing incumbents should be treated in the most liberal manner." This resolution was opposed by three classes of persons: First, by those who desire the existing settlement to be maintained. Second, by those who, though they object to the Imperial Act of 1840, and seek its repeal, admit, nevertheless, certain claims on the part of the Protestant clergy under the Constitutional Act of 1791. And lastly, by those who are unwilling to recognize even the claims of existing incumbents. It was carried on a division by a majority of two only; the numbers being 36 for, and 34 against it.

3. I deeply regret the revival of agitation on this subject, of which Lord Sydenham truly observed, that it had been in Upper Canada the one all-absorbing and engrossing topic of interest, and for years the principal cause of the discontent and disturbance which had arisen, and under which the province had labored. The intervention of the Imperial Parliament in 1840 was doubtless prompted by a desire to settle on terms which should be equitable and generally satisfactory, a question which had for so many years disturbed the peace of the colony. While the principle, however, of an establishment was abandoned by the Imperial Act 3 and 4 Vict., chap. 78, which admitted all denominations to share in the proceeds of the Clergy Reserves, advantages were given by it to the established Churches of England and Scotland in the distribution of the funds which render them still objects of envy. This feeling has been increased, as regards the Church of Scotland, by the large secession from its ranks, which the Free Church movement has occasioned. I much fear that the result will justify the disinclination which Lord John Russell appears, from the first, to have entertained to any legislation by the Imperial Parliament upon this question. It is an evil of no small magnitude on a subject of this nature, that while the more violent and unscrupulous of the opponents of the existing settlement are enabled to create a prejudice against it, by representing it to be the result of Imperial interference in a matter of provin-

cial concern, its friends are tempted rather to endeavor to influence opinion in England than to resort to measures which may strengthen their position in the colony.

I have, &c.,
(Signed) ELGIN AND KINCARDINE.

The Right Hon. The Earl Grey,
&c., &c., &c.

In due course Earl Grey informed the Governor General, in reply, that, " consistently with the principles on which they have " always held that the Government of Canada ought to be con- " ducted, it was impossible to advise her Majesty to refuse to " comply with the prayer of the address of the Assembly." In a later despatch, Earl Grey acquainted the Governor General with the circumstances under which " Her Majesty's Government are " compelled to postpone to another session the introduction of the " bill." Satisfied with Earl Grey's reply, Mr. Price moved in the session of 1851 the following resolution :—

"*Resolved*,—That an humble address be presented to Her Most Gracious Majesty, thanking her Majesty for the gracious manner in which she has been pleased to receive the address of this House of last session on the subject of the Clergy Reserves, and to assure her Majesty of the great satisfaction which it has afforded to this House and the Province at large to learn, from the despatch of the Right Honorable Earl Grey, her Majesty's Principal Secretary of State for the Colonies, communicating her Majesty's gracious reception of the said address, that it has appeared to her Majesty's Imperial Ministers that such address ought to be acceded to, and that they would accordingly be prepared to recommend to the Imperial Parliament that an act should be framed giving to the Provincial Legislature full authority to make such alterations as they may think fit in the existing arrangements with regard to those Reserves, provided that existing interests are respected."

Mr. Henry John Boulton moved in amendment—

"That the most direct, clear, and satisfactory mode of conveying to the Queen and her Imperial Parliament the wishes of the Legislature of Canada, on the subject of the Clergy Reserves, would be to pass an act containing all the provisions intended to be adopted, with a clause suspending its operation until it shall have received the express sanction of the British Parliament—a course which was most satisfactorily followed upon the subject of the Civil List in 1846.

"*Resolved*,—That the Hon. Messrs. Price, Baldwin, Cayley, Morrison, and the mover, be a committee to draught and report a bill to this House accordingly."

There were two decided objections in the opinion of Mr. Baldwin, and those with whom he acted, to Mr. Boulton's amendment. 1st. It was well known that there were strong objections in England, and especially in the House of Lords, to the secularization of the Clergy Reserves. It was believed that—while in deference to the constitutional right of the Canadian Parliament to legislate as it saw fit on a local question, Parliament might consent to repeal the Imperial act and to place the disposition of the Reserves in the hands of the local Legislature—it would be infinitely more difficult to procure its sanction to an act containing all the provisions intended to be adopted; in other words, provisions for the secularization of the Reserves. No one can read the despatches of Earl Grey without being convinced of his sincerity. One of the reasons assigned for postponing the introduction of the bill for the repeal of the Imperial act, was the wish of the Government " to bring the measure forward in the manner best calculated to " ensure success."

Lord Derby had, as is well known, a majority of supporters in the House of Lords, and the subsequent policy of that nobleman's Government may be taken as affording proof that if Lord Grey had introduced his bill in 1851 it would have been defeated. No one who impartially studies the parliamentary proceedings of 1851 can arrive at any other conclusion than that the postponement of the Clergy Reserve Bill in that year was a wise determination on the part of Lord John Russell's Government, then in a tottering position. It would have been most unwise for the Canadian Reformers to have placed new difficulties in the way of a minister pledged to use his endeavors to comply with the address to the Crown which all had concurred in a year before. But secondly. Had an attempt been made to legislate in accordance with public opinion it would have involved the breaking up of the administration. Mr. Lafontaine, Mr. Cauchon, Mr. Chauveau and other Lower Canadians had voted against the resolution of Mr. Price, which affirmed that " no religious " denomination can be held to have such vested interests in the " revenue derived from the proceeds of the said Clergy Reserves " as should prevent further legislation with reference to the "disposal of them," and would have voted against any bill that Mr. Boulton's committee would have reported. On the other hand, Mr. Lafontaine was strongly in favor of the settlement of the question by the Canadian Parliament, and was willing to go heartily for the repeal of the Imperial Act. It was not deemed prudent to precipitate a disruption of the Reform party on a question on which, by general admission, it was out of the power of the Canadian Parliament to legislate. Mr. Boulton's amendment was lost on a division of 5 to 52. Mr. Wm. Lyon Mackenzie moved an amendment, the division on which was 4 to 56. Mr. Cayley and Mr. Sherwood moved amendments in a Conservative sense, which were lost—13 to 50 and 10 to 46, and the address was finally carried by 45 to 16, the minority including four or five Reformers with the Conservatives. Such was the action of the House in 1851. During that session, Mr. Baldwin resigned as a member of the administration, and Mr. Lafontaine announced his contemplated withdrawal from public life. A general election was at hand, and prior to that the Governor-General entrusted me with the formation of a new administration, which I formed on the clear understanding with Mr. Morin that the secularization of the Clergy Reserves would be a cabinet question. At this critical moment, the Hon. George Brown addressed a series of letters to me, in which he stated his reasons for opposing the new administration. I have already made a brief quotation from one, and shall add an extract specially relating to the Clergy Reserves:—

THE CLERGY RESERVES.

"I now come to the great question of the Clergy Reserves. I think you erred greatly in not having it settled with your French Canadian colleagues that this was to be treated as a Ministerial question, ere you assented to the Rebellion Losses Bill. I do not doubt, however, that you entertained the full conviction, until immediately preceding the Session of 1850, that Mr. Lafontaine and his adherents would go with you cordially on that subject. When they refused to do so, it became a question whether you ought to resign. I had no doubt, at the opening of Parliament, in May, 1850, that Mr. Price and you were desirous of settling the Reserves, as the Upper Canada Reform party demand, and that you were much disappointed that you could not have that settlement made a Ministerial question; and I fully agreed with you that, in the then state of the question, the Provincial Parliament had not power of itself to set aside the Imperial Act of 1840, and that the consent of the Imperial Parliament must be had to any Canadian legislation on the subject. I also agreed with you that, as your colleagues were willing to go with you for an Address to the Crown to restore the control of the Reserves to the Provincial Parliament; and as the difference between you arose, not on the steps you proposed taking, but on the argument on which such control should be claimed—and on the future appropriation of the lands when obtained—you were not called upon to resign; but were justified in carrying your preliminary Address to the Crown as an open question, and taking your stand when the practical question came up, What shall be done with the lands? It is still quite clear that this was the right ground; for if you had then resigned, no advance would have been made on the question until after a new election, then two years off; and you would thereby have lost the opportunity, which no true Reformer doubted you would meantime have seized, to place the representation and suffrage on such footing, ere the election, as would free the Upper Canada Liberals from their position of dependence on their Lower Canada allies. I also agreed with the contents of Mr. Price's resolutions, though decidedly preferring Mr. Morrison's amendment, asking the control of the Reserves, free from any restriction. I opposed the proposition to pass an ordinary Bill settling the question, because I did not agree with the friends of that measure when they contended that the Act of 1840 had not repealed the power given us to legislate by the Act of 1791. With you, I considered that the Act of 1840 did bar Provincial legislation, and that to proceed in the face of it would bring us into collision with the Home Government. Moreover, I considered that such a Bill must receive, as all Bills have to receive, the assent of the Mother Country ere becoming law, and that this would be much more easily obtained by a courteous, though firm, representation of facts, and invitation to action, than by rudely attempting to force an Act of our own down the Imperial throat.

Up to the meeting of Parliament this year, therefore, I was with you on the Reserve question, and did not doubt your perfect good faith in regard to it. That opinion has undergone a very great change in consequence of your subsequent proceedings; and though I do not doubt that were you to carry out your own convictions you would act as the cause of justice demands, I am satisfied you are prepared to sacrifice your principles and your party, even on this question, to subserve your own ends.

The speech from the throne at the opening of the Session was calculated to excite strong suspicion as to your earnestness on the subject. In the coldest manner possible, it merely alluded to Lord Grey's reply to the address of the House—expressed no feeling—indicated no further movement on the subject! The despatches were, however, promised to be communicated, and when received it appeared that the Home Government assented to the demand of the people of Canada, and would at some future day transfer back the power of disposing of the Reserves to the Provincial Parliament. No time was fixed, however,—no hurry about the matter seemed to be conceived necessary, and suspicion was consequently aroused that Lord Grey had received a hint that prompt action would be inconvenient for the Provincial Cabinet. These suspicions received ten-fold strength when it appeared that in sending Mr. Price's resolutions to the Colonial Office, the Governor General had been advised by you and your colleagues to use language in the despatch accompanying them calculated seriously to injure the cause at home. In this despatch his Lordship wrote that he "*deeply regrets the revival of agitation on this (the Clergy Reserve) subject,*"—and he goes on thus:—

"It is an evil of no small magnitude on a subject of this nature, that *while the more violent and unscrupulous of the opponents of the existing settlement* are enabled to create a prejudice against it by representing it to be the result of Imperial interference in a matter of provincial concern, *its friends* are tempted rather to endeavor to influence opinion in England than *to resort to measures which may strengthen their position in the colony.*"

Well did it become you, indeed, to pronounce the Reformers of Upper Canada "violent and unscrupulous," because they sought to abolish an "existing settlement"—bless your new-born fastidiousness!—by declaiming against which you raised yourself to your present position! Who was ever more "violent and unscrupulous" than yourself on this or any other question? Well it suited you, forsooth, to preach down such language to the Voluntaries of Upper Canada, who placed you on your perch! And let me not forget your timely hint to the "friends" of the Reserves, to "*resort to measures which may strengthen their position in the colony!*" No man can doubt that this recommendation was thrown to Bishop Strachan and his coadjutors here and in England designedly and of forethought; quite certain is it that the clerical agitation—the "church unions," the "pastoral addresses," and the "lay delegations"—which immediately sprang up throughout the land, were the fruit of this despatch from a Reform Administration; and as little doubtful is it now that in this whole affair you were purposely holding out the right hand of fellowship to High Churchism, and telling her, as you did afterwards by votes and speeches not to be mistaken, We, the present Ministry, are not among "the violent and unscrupulous" opponents of "the Lord Bishop of Toronto"—we are not among the "Pharisaical brawlers" of Upper Canada—we are in favour of "vested rights," and won't suffer them to be touched—we "deeply regret" the "strong feeling" against the Church of England, but will "endeavour to do justice to her"—we will get the Home Government to throw the Reserve question over the election, and meantime you can try to raise a storm in the country—we mean to keep office, and circumstances may occur which will cast us into the same boat with you!"

I shall as briefly as possible offer some explanatory remarks on the foregoing extract. Though the letter is personally addressed to me, Mr. Baldwin was my leader in 1849, and he, if any one, "erred" in not making his support of the Rebellion Losses Bill conditional on Mr. Lafontaine's adhesion to the secularization of the Clergy Reserves. I am perfectly certain that nothing would have induced Mr. Baldwin to adopt such a line of action, and I am equally certain that Mr. Lafontaine would not have sacrificed his convictions on one measure to secure support for another. Such a proceeding would have been justly characterized as log-rolling. The letter proceeds to justify all our policy on the Clergy Reserve question, the writer declaring, "up to the meeting of Parliament this year, therefore, I was with you on the Reserve question, and did not doubt your perfect good faith in regard to it." The question then is, are the grounds stated by the writer adequate to justify the "*suspicions*" which induced him to declare himself satisfied that I was prepared to sacrifice my principles and my party to subserve my own ends? There was suspicion aroused that Lord Grey " had received a hint that prompt action would be inconvenient to the Provincial Cabinet." It is difficult, of course, to defend oneself from suspicions. There never was even the shadow of a ground for them; and Lord Grey, an English nobleman of unblemished honour, declared, in a despatch made public at the time, that the chief cause for delay was a desire to ensure the success of the measure. Lord Elgin's reputation stands, I think, sufficiently high to shield him from the imputation of such a trick,—and Messrs. Lafontaine and Baldwin, then the leaders of the Administration, were not men to whom such practices were imputed by those most in opposition to them. The speech from the throne made precisely the proper reference to the subject. It promised the despatch in reply to the address from the House, and left the House to take the proper action, which it did in due course, by assuring Her Majesty of their satisfaction at the assurance given them that the prayer of their address would be complied with. But then the *suspicions* received ten-fold strength from the Governor's despatch transmitting the address for which I was made responsible, although it has never been held, to my knowledge, by any Canadian statesman, that the Governor General of Canada writes his despatches to the Secretary of State, on the advice of his Ministers. Earl Grey had a right to Lord Elgin's unbiassed opinion of the address of the House of Assembly, which he transmitted, and which in terms sufficiently explicit, conveyed the wishes of that body. Lord Elgin's personal opinions were certainly against secularization. I am not of opinion, however, that the despatch was calculated to injure the popular cause, and the decision of the Imperial Government is the best proof that it was not. Be that as it may, I entirely disclaim all responsibility for the Governor's despatch, and yet my condemnation avowedly rested on a document which I solemnly declare I never saw until about the time when it became public. It never entered into the imagination of Mr. Lafontaine or Mr. Baldwin, or of any other statesman with whom I have been associated, that the administration was politically responsible for the Governor's despatches to the Secretary of State, conveying his opinions on questions of policy. I must proceed to the action of the new administration. Early in 1852 I visited England as one of a deputation on the subject of the Intercolonial Railway. I sailed for England on the 4th of March of that year, shortly after my return from the Maritime Provinces, whither I went in the preceding January, accompanied by the Honbles. Col. Taché and John Young. On the 25th February, a memorandum was agreed to by the members of the Government as to pressing the repeal of the Imperial Act, although no doubt was entertained as to the intentions of the Government. It was not until my arrival in England that I learned that the Whig Government had resigned and had been succeeded by Lord Derby, who made his exposition of policy on 27th February. I felt the necessity of having my hands strengthened, and immediately communicated with my colleagues, and I shall proceed to submit the various documents commencing with my letter enclosing the minute of Council :—

Copy of a letter from F. HINCKS, ESQ., *to the Right Honorable Sir* JOHN S. PAKINGTON, *Bart.*

Morley's Hotel, London, May 3, 1852.

SIR,—I have the honor to enclose a copy of an approved Report of the Committee of the Executive Council of Canada, dated the

7th ultimo, which I received by the last mail. I have learned through the medium of the public journals, that Her Majesty's Government has determined to take no action in the question of the Clergy Reserves during the present session of Parliament; and however much I may regret that decision, I am well aware that, under the circumstances, it is irrevocable. I have already had an opportunity of urging, during the interview with which you were good enough to honor me, the importance of settling this long vexed question as speedily as possible. It was my duty to state that the number of those who insist on the present settlement is very small, and I may now add that one of the leading opposition newspapers in Upper Canada, and in the interest of the Church of England, has come out distinctly for a new scheme of distribution. I would press on Her Majesty's Government more formally what I have already urged in my conversation with you, that if, as has been alleged, the present Canadian Parliament is favorable to the views of the Church of England, it is surely the best time for that church to procure a settlement that will be regarded as constitutional. I can assure Her Majesty's Government, with the utmost sincerity, that there will be no end to agitation in Canada if the attempt be made to settle this question permanently according to the public opinion of England instead of that of the province itself; and I may add that it is well known that many who are opponents of the secularization of the Clergy Reserves are on constitutional grounds in favor of a settlement by the Provincial Parliament. I believe that, after the assurance given by the late Government, it will be found impossible to protract very long the repeal of the Imperial Act; and I have no hesitation in affirming that no interests will suffer more by delay than those of the Church of England. If Her Majesty's Government desire, before determining on their line of action on this question, to ascertain the views of the present Canadian Parliament, I would respectfully beg to be informed of their decision.

   I have, &c.,
       (Signed)   FRANCIS HINCKS.
Sir J. S. Pakington, Bart.,
 &c., &c., &c.

(Enclosure.)

Extract from a Report of a Committee of the Honorable the Executive Council on Matters of State, dated 7th April, 1852, approved by his Excellency the Governor-General in Council on the same day.

The Committee have had under consideration the memorandum of the President of the Committee of Council on the propriety of instructing the Honorable the Inspector-General to ascertain the views of Her Majesty's Government on the subject of a repeal of the Imperial Act 3 & 4 Vict., c. 78, in conformity with the addresses to Her Most Gracious Majesty from both branches of the Canadian Legislature at its last session, on the subject of the Clergy Reserves.

The assurances of Her Majesty's late Government that such action would be taken, had prepared the people of Canada to expect that no further delay would take place in meeting their just wishes upon a question of such paramount importance to them; the Committee therefore recommend that their colleague the Inspector-General, while in England, be requested by the provincial secretary to seek an interview with Her Majesty's Ministers, and represent to them the importance of carrying out the pledges of their predecessors on the subject of the Clergy Reserves, and thus empower the colonial legislature to deal with the question in accordance with the well-understood wishes of the people of Canada.

Certified.

(Signed)   WM. H. LEE.

The Hon. the Provincial Secretary,
&c., &c., &c.

Copy of a letter from the EARL OF DESART *to* F. HINCKS, ESQ.

Downing Street, May 7, 1852.

SIR,—I am directed by Secretary Sir John Pakington to acknowledge your letter of the 3rd instant, transmitting an extract from an approved Report of a Committee of the Executive Council of Canada, dated 7th April, instructing you to represent to Her Majesty's Ministers the importance of carrying out the pledges of their predecessors on the subject of the Clergy Reserves.

Sir J. Pakington desires me to inform you, that until the receipt of your communication he was not aware of the existence of the Report of which you now send him a copy, Lord Elgin not having as yet transmitted it to this department. Being thus without information that you were officially instructed to communicate with Her Majesty's Government on that particular subject, Sir J. Pakington did not think it necessary to announce to you their determination upon it, as he unquestionably would have done if he had been aware that your missson to this country was connected with it. I am now directed by Sir J. Pakington to enclose to you a copy of the despatch which he addressed to Lord Elgin on the 22nd ultimo, communicating the decision of Her Majesty's Government.

I have, &c.,

(Signed)   DESART.

Copy of a Despatch from SIR JOHN S. PAKINGTON, Bart., *to the* EARL OF ELGIN AND KINCARDINE.

Downing Street, April 22, 1852.

MY LORD,—By a Despatch of my predecessor, Earl Grey, of the 11th July last, you were informed that Her Majesty's then servants found themselves compelled to postpone to another session the introduction into Parliament of a Bill giving to the Canadian Legislature authority to alter the existing arrangement with regard to the Clergy Reserves.

2. With reference to that intimation, I have now to inform you that it is not the intention of Her Majesty's present advisers to propose such a measure to Parliament this session.

3. They have, in the first place, taken into consideration that, since any opinion upon this difficult subject was expressed by the Legislature of Canada, a general election has taken place in the Province, and it is as yet uncertain what the views of the new Assembly as to the disposal of the Clergy Reserves may be.

4. But, independently of that circumstance, Her Majesty's Government feel serious doubts how far they would be able to give their consent and support to an arrangement, the result of which would too probably be the diversion to other purposes of the only public fund, except that devoted to the endowment of the Roman Catholic Church, which now exists for the support of Divine worship and religious instruction in the colony.

5. While it appears to Her Majesty's Government that, under the distribution authorized by the Clergy Reserves Act, 3 & 4 Vict. c. 78, of the proceeds of the sales of the reserved lands, no ground is left for reasonable jealousy or complaint of undue favour to particular religious denominations, they think it may possibly be desirable, on account of the changes which may be effected in the character of the population through extensive immigration or other causes, that the distribution in question should from time to time be reconsidered.

6. Any proposals of such a nature Her Majesty's Government would be willing to entertain; but they are of opinion that they could only regard any measure which would place it in the power of an accidental majority of the colonial legislature, however small, to divert for ever from its sacred object the fund arising from that portion of the public lands of Canada which, almost from the period of the British conquest of that Province, has been set apart for the religious instruction of the people, with the most serious doubt and hesitation how far they should be justified in advising Her Majesty to give Her consent to such an enactment.

7. These views on the part of Her Majesty's Government, with respect to a proposal so deeply and permanently affecting the interests of Canada, cannot but derive additional strength from the numerous petitions, having many thousand signatures, which

have been addressed both to the Queen and to the Parliament of the United Kingdom, praying that the existing Act relating to the Clergy Reserves may continue in force.—I have, &c.

      (Signed,) JOHN S. PAKINGTON.
Governor the Right Hon.   ⎫
The Earl of Elgin and Kincardine, ⎬
 &c.,   &c.,   &c.   ⎭

Copy of a letter from F. HINCKS, ESQ., *to the Right Honorable Sir* JOHN S. PAKINGTON, *Bart.*

      Morley's Hotel, London, May 10, 1852.

SIR,—I have the honor to acknowledge the receipt of a letter from the Earl of Desart, dated the 7th instant, enclosing a copy of your despatch to Governor-General the Earl of Elgin and Kincardine, dated the 22nd ultimo, communicating the decision of Her Majesty's Government on the subject of the Canada Clergy Reserves, and I have to express my grateful acknowledgments therefor. It is probable that as the approved Report of the Committee of the Executive Council of Canada was sent to me for the purpose of being delivered to Her Majesty's Government, it was deemed unnecessary by his Excellency the Governor-General to transmit another copy; but you will, I think, find on enquiry, that his Excellency has communicated to you a copy of a memorandum agreed to at a meeting of the members of the Council on the 25th February, prior to my departure, by which I was instructed " to press upon the consideration of Her Majesty's Government the importance of procuring the assent of the Imperial Parliament as soon as possible, to a Bill for repealing the Imperial Act, 3 & 4 Vict. c. 78, providing for the sale of the Clergy Reserves in Canada, and for the distribution of the proceeds thereof, as prayed for by addresses from both houses of the provincial Parliament, and for authorizing the provincial Parliament to legislate on the subject of those Reserves."

I trust that the existence of these instructions, followed up as they have been by the approved Report of Council, which I had the honor to transmit in my letter of the 3rd instant, will be a sufficient apology for my offering some remarks on your despatch of the 22nd ultimo, which shall be made in a spirit of the highest respect to Her Majesty's Government. Had the addresses from the two houses of the Canadian Legislature prayed for any particular distribution of the income arising from the Clergy Reserve Fund, there most unquestionably would have been grave objections to any Imperial action to be founded on the opinions of a Parliament which had ceased to exist. But I would respectfully urge, that there can be no reasonable ground for doubt, that the great majority of the people of Canada desire that this question, which is one of local interest, should be disposed of by their own Parliament. I need not, however, press this point further, because I am well aware that legislation during the present session of the Imperial Parliament is now out of the question, and that before any further action could be taken by Her Majesty's Government, the new Canadian Parliament will have an opportunity of expressing its views on the subject. But I am bound by a sense of duty to Her Majesty to express to Her confidential advisers, that it is with the most serious alarm that I have read the concluding portion of your despatch. Most devotedly attached as I am to the maintenance of the subsisting connexion between the mother country and the British American colonies, I cannot view without grave apprehension the prospect of collision between Her Majesty's Government and the Parliament of Canada, on a question regarding which such strong feelings prevail among the great mass of the population. Such a difficulty is the more, to be regretted, because the question of the Clergy Reserves is the only one, so far as I am aware, at all likely to lead to collision. It happens, most unfortunately, that public opinion in England differs very widely from that in Canada, on questions at all partaking of a. religious character; and as the people of Canada are convinced that they are better judges than any parties in England can be, of what measures will best conduce to the peace and welfare of the province, Her Majesty's Government will, I trust, perceive that the danger which I apprehend is at least deserving of the most grave consideration. I cannot have the slightest doubt that the members of Her Majesty's Government are actuated by the most earnest desire to promote the best interests of Canada, and that if they could be brought to believe that I have given a faithful account of the state of public opinion there, they would be disposed to yield their own wishes for the sake of the peace of the colony. I am quite ready to acknowledge the high respectability of the petitioners against the repeal of the Clergy Reserves Act. The bishops, clergy, and an influential portion of the laity of the Church of England, the clergy and a portion of the laity of the Church of Scotland, are doubtless in favor of the present settlement, which, indeed, confers on the Church of Scotland an income wholly beyond its requirements in Canada; while the majority of the Presbyterian population neither receive any share of the endowment, nor desire to participate in it. While, however, I admit the respectability of the petitioners, I think that I am justified in affirming that they do not represent anything like a majority of the population of Canada; indeed, the very fact that they on all occasions endeavour to accomplish their wishes by appealing not to their own representatives in Parliament, but to the Imperial Parliament, is conclusive proof that they are themselves conscious that their views are not in accordance with public opinion in Canada. I forbear from entering into the consideration of the probable action of the Canadian Legislature on the Clergy Reserves question, because I am anxious to impress on Her Majesty's Government that, although there may be wide differences of opinion among the opponents of the present arrangement as to the best mode of settling the question, a vast majority of the people are agreed as to the necessity of its being effected by provincial legislation; and I am aware that some of the best friends of the Church of England question the soundness of the policy which has influenced the promoters of the petitions lately presented to Parliament to look for support to their views in England, instead of using their legitimate influence over public opinion in Canada. I do not by any means desire to conceal from Her Majesty's Government that, saving always the right of existing incumbents, a very strong feeling prevails, especially in Upper Canada, in favour of the secularization of the Clergy Reserves; but I ought not to omit reminding them that, although it is true that the portion of public lands known as Clergy Reserves was set apart for the religious instruction of the people at a very early period, and when there were very few inhabitants in the colony, it is likewise true that power was expressly given to the Provincial Legislature " to vary or repeal " the clauses in the Act 31 George III., setting apart these lands; that successive Houses of Assembly remonstrated against giving effect to them, and that so firmly were the advisers of His late Majesty King William IV. impressed with the necessity of getting rid of this most perplexing question, that Secretary Viscount Goderich, in a despatch dated 21st November, 1831, communicated the Royal instructions that a bill, framed in England, should be submitted to the Provincial Legislature for the purpose of getting rid entirely of the endowment. The people of Canada know well the cause of the failure in carrying out the gracious intentions of His late Majesty, as well as their own repeatedly expressed wishes. The opinions of the mass of the people have never wavered during the last twenty-five years, although circumstances have from time to time induced them to pause in their efforts, in order to concentrate public opinion on questions more deeply affecting their constitutional rights. I cannot, therefore, conceive that any action which the Canadian Parliament may take of the nature referred to in the despatch, could be correctly designated as the result of an accidental majority. All the great questions which have been settled in England during the last fifty years might be said, with equal justice, to have been carried by accidental majorities; and if a supposition on the part of Her Majesty's Government that any majority in the Canadian Parliament expressing views antagonistic to their own was an accidental one, were deemed a sufficient ground for resisting that majority, I would most respectfully submit that there would be no security whatever for constitutional government. I am well convinced that Her Majesty's advisers have every disposition to attach due weight to the clearly expressed opinion of the people of Canada, and I am therefore anxious to remind them of, and to urge upon their consideration, the past history of the Clergy Reserves question, which I have endeavoured to glance at as briefly as possible. There is a passage in the despatch to the Earl of Elgin which seems to me calculated to lead to some misconception. I refer to the paragraph describing the Clergy Reserves as the only "public fund, except that devoted to the endowment of the Roman Catholic Church." I am not aware that any public fund has ever been devoted to the endowment of the Roman Catholic Church in Canada. Whatever property may be in possession of Roman Catholics has been obtained principally by private donation or bequest, although in some cases there were additional grants from the French Crown, which were secured to the possessors at the Conquest. These grants were made to communities consisting of ecclesiastics or religious ladies, either for charitable or educational purposes, or for the conversion of the Indians. If I am correct in this statement, as I believe that I am, I most respectfully submit that such grants, as those to which I have referred, bear no analogy to the Clergy Reserves, and can scarcely be considered as a public fund devoted to the endowment of the Roman Catholic Church. I should not discharge my duty to Her Majesty's Government were I not to state to them with perfect frankness my views on another paragraph in the despatch. I refer to that in which it is intimated that Her Majesty's Government would be willing to entertain a proposal for reconsidering the mode of distributing the income of the Clergy Reserves. I have no hesitation in stating it as my conviction that the Canadian Parliament will not invite the legislation of the Imperial Parliament regarding the distribution of a local fund. Any such proposition would be received as one for the violation of the most sacred constitutional rights of the people. I am therefore fully convinced that the future action of the Canadian Parliament will be essentially of the same character with that which has been already taken. I can assure you, Sir, that it is with deep regret that I find myself compelled by a sense of public duty to urge upon you views which I fear will not meet the approbation of Her Majesty's Government; but I trust that I have succeeded in doing so in a respectful manner; and I feel assured that they will receive the consideration which the importance of the subject demands, and that Her Majesty's advisers will be guided in their final decision by what they believe to be for the best interests of Canada.

I have, &c.,

(Signed,)   FRANCIS HINCKS.

Sir J. S. Pakington, Bart.,
&c., &c., &c.

Copy of Letter from the EARL OF DESART *to* FRANCIS HINCKS, Esq.:

Downing street, May 17, 1852.

SIR,—I am directed by Secretary Sir John Pakington to acknowledge your letter of the 10th of this month, on the subject of the decision of Her Majesty's Government as to the Clergy Reserves question, and to thank you for the representations which you have made to them on this and other subjects affecting the views and interests of the people of Canada, on which they are fully sensible of the value of your opinion.

2. I am to add that Sir John Pakington has not been able to find in the records of this department any trace of the memorandum agreed to by the Executive Council on the 25th February last, to which your letter refers, having been communicated to his predecessor or himself.

I have, &c.,

(Signed,) DESART.

F. Hincks, Esq.

During the ensuing session of the Canadian Parliament, it became the duty of the writer to move the following series of resolutions:—

1. That whatever differences of opinion may exist among the people of Canada as to the best mode of disposing of the revenues derived from the lands known as Clergy Reserves, the great mass of the people will ever maintain the principle recognized by the Right Honorable the Earl Grey, then Her Majesty's Principal Secretary of State for the Colonies, in his despatch of 27th January, 1851, to the Right Honorable the Earl of Elgin and Kincardine, that the question whether the existing arrangement "is to be maintained or altered is one so exclusively affecting the people of Canada, that its decision ought not to be withdrawn from the Provincial Legislature, to which it properly belongs to regulate all matters concerning the domestic interest of the province."

2. That while the people of Canada are devotedly attached to Her Majesty's person and Government, and most anxious to maintain inviolate the connexion which binds them to the great empire over which she rules, yet this House is bound by a high sense of duty to inform Her Majesty, that the refusal on the part of the Imperial Parliament to comply with the just demand of the representatives of the Canadian people on a matter exclusively affecting their own interests, will be viewed as a violation of their constitutional rights, and will lead to deep and wide-spread dissatisfaction among Her Majesty's Canadian subjects.

3. That this House is well aware that attempts have been made to induce Her Majesty's Imperial Ministers to believe that the

present representatives of the people of Canada entertain opinions on the subject of the repeal of the Clergy Reserves Act different from those expressed by the late Parliament.

4. That this House confidently hopes, that when Her Majesty's Ministers shall be convinced that the opinions of the people of Canada and of their representatives on this subject are unaltered and unalterable, they will consent to give effect to the promise made by their predecessors; and this House is confirmed in this hope by the suggestion in the despatch of the Right Honourable Sir John Pakington, that Her Majesty's Ministers are prepared to recommend amendments to the Imperial Clergy Reserves Act, with a view to satisfy the wishes of the Canadian people.

5. That this House can scarcely doubt that, the principle of amending the present Act being admitted, Her Majesty's Ministers will yield to the strong feeling which pervades the Canadian people, that any new legislative enactments regarding the Clergy Reserves should be framed by their own representatives, instead of by the Imperial Parliament, which, being necessarily unacquainted with the state of public opinion in Canada, cannot be expected to concur in a measure that will give permanent satisfaction to its inhabitants.

6. That this House desires to assure Her Majesty, that in thus giving expression to the public opinion of the country, it is actuated by the strongest feelings of loyalty to Her Majesty, and by a sincere desire to prevent those lamentable consequences which must be the result of a collision between the Imperial and Provincial Parliaments, on a question on which very strong feelings are known to prevail among the people of this Province.

The Address founded on the above resolutions was received in England very shortly before the resignation of the Earl of Derby; but a draft despatch, which had been prepared by Sir John Pakington for transmission by the mail, 16th December, 1852, was laid before Parliament, and as Sir John moved for its production, justice to him requires its insertion here.

Draft of a Despatch from Sir John S. Pakington *to Governor-General the* Earl of Elgin, *prepared for transmission by mail of 16th December,* 1852.

Downing Street, December, 1852.

My Lord,—I have had the honour to receive your Lordship's despatch,* No. 85, of the 22nd September, forwarding an address to the Queen from the Commons of Canada, in Provincial Parliament assembled, on the subject of the Clergy Reserves.

---

* Page 7 of Papers relative to "Clergy Reserves, Canada," presented to both Houses of Parliament, by command of Her Majesty, 11th February, 1853.

2. I have laid this Address before Her Majesty, who was pleased to receive it very graciously.

3. It is with sincere regret that Her Majesty's Government feel themselves unable to advise Her Majesty to comply with the wishes of the Assembly, for the introduction of a Bill into the Imperial Parliament, to repeal the Act 3 and 4 Vic. c. 78.

4. In arriving reluctantly at this conclusion, Her Majesty's advisers disclaim any intention of "violating the constitutional rights" of the Canadian Parliament. On the contrary, they regard those rights with the high respect which is justly due to them, and they fully and distinctly recognize both the justice and the propriety of the general rule that in those dependencies of the British Crown, which enjoy the advantages of representative institutions, questions which affect exclusively local interests, should be decided and dealt with by the Local Government and Legislature.

5. But Her Majesty's Government are not less clearly of opinion that the question of the repeal of the Imperial Act 3 and 4 Vict. c. 78, involves interests, and is connected with circumstances, which make it fairly an exception to this general rule.

6. It is the earnest desire of Her Majesty's Government, not only to avoid any serious "difference of opinion" with the Legislature of Canada, but to act with them, if possible, in friendly concert, upon a subject of such great and enduring importance to the Canadian people, especially of the Upper Province.

7. Her Majesty's Government desire to call the attention of the Commons of Canada to the circumstances under which the Imperial Act was passed.

8. After a long period of agitation, and frequent attempts at legislation on the part of the Upper Canadian Assembly, an Act was passed by the Parliament of that Province for placing the disposal of the Clergy Reserves in the hands of the Imperial Parliament. This Act was not confirmed, for reasons stated in Lord John Russell's despatch to Lord Sydenham of the 7th February, 1839. Another Act, providing for the sale and disposal of the Clergy Reserves, was subsequently passed by the Provincial Legislature. This Act would have received the Royal Assent, but for a legal objection which was found to be insuperable.

9. In consequence of the legal difficulty to the confirmation by the Crown of the Provincial Act, the Act 3 and 4 Vict. c. 78, similar in principle, though differing in detail from the Act sent from Canada, was passed by the Imperial Parliament.

10. Her Majesty's Government cannot fail to remember that not only was the Imperial Act similar in principle to the Provincial Act, but that the former was passed and regarded at the same time, both in Canada and this country, as a final settlement of a long agitated and most difficult question; and the settlement of which had moreover been pressed upon the Imperial Govern-

ment by successive Governors of the Canadian Provinces, and by the general wish of the Canadian people.

11. Her Majesty's Government would further remind the House of Assembly that the generally admitted necessity of permanently settling this long debated question, had reference, not only to the manifest evils of prolonged agitation, but also to the circumstances under which the reunion of the two Provinces of Canada was then about to take place.

12. It was held, and in the opinion of Her Majesty's Government it was wisely held, to be of paramount importance, that a permanent settlement of the Clergy Reserve question should precede the Act of reunion.

13. In considering, therefore, how far it is right or expedient to reopen this question, it is impossible for Her Majesty's advisers to overlook the fact, that since it has been decided, the two Provinces, with a population for the most part distinct both in race and religion, have been united under one representative Government.

14. Her Majesty's advisers have pleasure in expressing their high sense of the loyalty and good feeling of the French-Canadian population of the Eastern Province. They have the satisfaction of believing that friendly feeling between the French and British population is steadily and constantly increasing; and they would deprecate, in the most earnest manner, any course of action on the part of the Provincial Parliament, which might have the least tendency to interrupt those amicable relations which now so happily subsist between the two races.

15. The French population of the Lower Province enjoy the blessing of an exemplary, a well educated, and a numerous priesthood, with ample endowments for the support of the priests, and for the maintenance of exclusive educational institutions.

16. From the period of the conquest of Canada till the present day, these endowments have been scrupulously respected.

17. Her Majesty's Government have no disposition to question the right or to impugn the motives of such of the representatives of the French population of the Eastern Province in the Canadian Parliament, as may deem it their duty to vote, either for the repeal of the Clergy Reserve Act, or for the secularization of the Clergy Reserves. But they feel a deep interest in the peace and welfare of all classes of Her Majesty's subjects in Canada, and with past struggles and contentions fresh in their recollection, they would earnestly press on the consideration of the Canadian Parliament, in no unfriendly spirit, whether there would not be danger of reviving feelings of animosity and discontent if the British inhabitants of the Upper Province were deprived by the Imperial Parliament of that fund for the support of Protestant worship which they have so long enjoyed, and which is now, whether for general or for missionary purposes, more than ever necessary.

18. I cannot thus communicate the views of Her Majesty's Government with respect to the Address of the House of Assembly which I have now to acknowledge, without repeating, in the most distinct terms, that nothing would be more painful to Her Majesty's advisers, or more at variance with their real feelings, than to be involved in any difference, or controversy with the Parliament of Canada, and that their only wish upon this difficult subject is to co-operate with the provincial authorities in promoting the permanent interests of all classes of Her Majesty's Canadian subjects.—I have, &c.

JOHN S. PAKINGTON.

It seems unnecessary to insert the Duke of Newcastle's despatch of 15th January, 1853, announcing the decision of the new Ministry to propose the repeal of the Imperial Act of 1840, which was successfully accomplished.

The decision of the Ministry, which was most fully concurred in by Lord Elgin, was not to propose legislation in the expiring Parliament; but there was some business of an urgent nature, particularly a Bill for giving effect to the Reciprocity treaty, that it was deemed advisable to dispose of before the dissolution. The House met in 1854, shortly after Lord Elgin's return from Washington, to which place he had been accompanied by the writer, as the representative of Canadian interests, during the negotiation of the treaty.

It soon became apparent that there would be an attempt to carry an amendment to the address in answer to the Governor-General's speech, in which the Conservatives, Clear Grits, and Rouges, could concur.

The following despatch from the Earl of Elgin to the Duke of Newcastle, contains a clear statement of the circumstances which led to a dissolution of the Canadian Parliament in 1854:

Copy of a Despatch from GOVERNOR-GENERAL THE EARL OF ELGIN AND KINCARDINE *to the* DUKE OF NEWCASTLE.

Government House, Quebec, June 22, 1854.

My Lord Duke,—I have the honor to enclose herewith the copy of a speech which I delivered from the throne this day in proroguing the Parliament of the province, and I beg at the same time to solicit your Grace's attention, while I state as succinctly as I can the grounds on which I formed the resolution which has given occasion for the delivery of this speech.

2. It may probably be in your Grace's recollection, that during the course of the last session of the Provincial Parliament, two Acts were passed, which had for their object to effect very material changes in the constitution of the popular branch of the Provincial Legislature. The former of these Acts raised the number of parliamentary representatives from 84 to 130, this addition to the House of Assembly being so effected as to equalize to a greater extent, than is now the case, population and representation. By the terms of the Constitutional Act, an Act of this nature could not become Law, unless it received in each branch of the Legislature, on the second and third readings, the support of at least two-thirds of the members. In the passage of this Act through the Provincial Parliament these conditions were complied with, and having received a notification of this fact by addresses in the mode prescribed by the Constitutional Act, I assented to it in Her Majesty's name on the 14th June, 1853.

3. The second of the Acts to which I have referred was entitled, "An Act to extend the Elective Franchise, and better to define "the Qualifications of Voters in certain Electoral Divisions, by "providing a system for the registration of Voters," and the intentions of the Act, as stated in the title, were duly carried out in its provisions.

4. While these proceedings were taking place in the Provincial Parliament, the Imperial Parliament passed an Act repealing the Imperial Statute which had regulated, since the year 1840, the distribution of the fund commonly known as the Clergy Reserve Fund of Canada, and leaving the future application of this fund, as a matter of local concern, to the determination of the Local Legislature. This important statute having been duly sanctioned by Her Majesty, reached me shortly before the prorogation of the Provincial Parliament.

5. The course which the Provincial Government ought to take at this conjuncture, whether in reference to the measures of constitutional change which had been enacted by the Local Parliament, or the Act respecting the Clergy Reserves which the Imperial Legislature had passed, became necessarily at an early period of the recess the subject of deliberation in the Provincial Cabinet. Some members of this body were strongly pledged to the secularization of the reserves, and it was believed that a proposal to carry out a measure of this description would be supported by a majority in the existing Assembly. After full consideration and discussion, however, my Executive Council arrived unanimously at the conclusion, that apart altogether from the merits of secularization, it would not be consistent with their duty to undertake to legislate upon this subject in the Parliament as then constituted. The Clergy Reserve question was one on which it was notorious that the public mind in Upper Canada, more especially, was much divided, and the Imperial statute on

the subject had been repealed for the express purpose of facilitating a settlement which would be final, and in accordance with the deliberate views and convictions of the people of the province. To attempt, therefore, to settle such a question in a Parliament which had been already declared by its own vote to be an imperfect representation of the people, and by the exercise of what might be deemed the influence of the Government, was a course of proceeding obviously open to serious objection. In these views of the Executive Council I entirely concurred.

6. An immediate dissolution of Parliament was apparently the readiest mode of escape from the perplexities to which I have referred. But here, again, a difficulty presented itself. In order to give time for the completion of the system of registration which formed part of the measure, the 1st day of January, 1855, had been fixed as the period at which the Act for extending the franchise should come into operation. To give it effect at an earlier time further legislation was required. It was, therefore, finally resolved by the Government that the then subsisting Parliament should be allowed to meet again for the purpose of legislating on this and other necessary matters, preparatory to a dissolution, after which the opinion of the Legislature, as constituted under the extended Representation and Franchise Acts, might be taken on those important questions, the settlement of which was anxiously desired by the people of the province.

7. In accordance with this determination, in my speech from the throne which I transmitted to your Grace by the last mail, with my Despatch No. 5, of the 15th instant, I recommended the passing of a law for bringing into early operation the Act of the preceding session which had extended the elective franchise, in order that a constitutional expression of opinion might be obtained as speedily as possible under the system of representation recently established, on the various important questions on which legislation was required, and I invited legislation in the then existing Parliament on two other subjects only; the one of these subjects being the Reciprocity Treaty, to give effect to which it was desirable that an Act of the Provincial Parliament should be passed without delay; and the other the Tariff, in which the prosperous condition of the revenue justified certain reductions.

8. The first amendment to the address was moved by the Honorable Mr. Sherwood, a leading member of the Conservative party, who objected to the late period at which the Parliament had been convened. The explanations on this head, however, were deemed sufficient by the majority of the Assembly, and the amendment was accordingly rejected by 40 votes to 29. Mr. Cauchon, a French Canadian member, then moved, that at the end of the fourth paragraph of the address in answer to the speech delivered at the opening of the session, the following

words should be inserted:—"That this House sees with regret "that his Excellency's Government do not intend to submit to "the Legislature during the present session a bill for the "immediate settlement of the Seigniorial question;" to which amendment Mr. Hartman, an Upper Canada member, of the Liberal party, moved as an amendment, to leave out all the words after "House," and add the following instead thereof:— "regret that his Excellency has not been advised to recommend "during the present session a measure for the secularization of "the Clergy Reserves, and also a measure for the abolition of the "Seigniorial tenure." The Ministerial and Conservative parties concurred in opposing this motion, which was accordingly defeated by a majority of 54 votes to 16. Mr. Sicotte, another French Canadian member, then moved that the words "or one "for the immediate settlement of the Clergy Reserves," should be carried to the end of Mr. Cauchon's amendment, and this motion was carried by 42 votes against 29; the Conservative members availing themselves of the ambiguity of the word "settlement," to join the party who were censuring the administration for not having introduced during the then session a bill for the secularization of the Clergy Reserves.

9. It will be obvious to your Grace, from the above statement of facts, that a most embarrassing situation was created by this vote. It pledged the then subsisting Parliament to settle the question of the Clergy Reserves, and it was carried by a combination of parties holding opposite views with respect to the terms on which the settlement should be effected. It was my decided opinion that no measure on this subject short of a measure of entire secularization could possibly have been carried through that House of Assembly, with the prospect, more especially, of an immediate dissolution hanging over the heads of its members. Against a measure of secularization carried under such circumstances the friends of religious endowments would, I conceived, have had good cause to complain. But if, on the other hand, out of the heterogeneous elements of which the majority was composed, I had been able to form a Conservative Administration, and with the aid of that Administration to pass a measure for perpetuating the endowment, I felt confident that in place of settling this vexed question, I should by so doing only have given the signal for renewed and more violent agitation. The advocates of secularization would never have admitted the permanency of a settlement effected by a Parliament so peculiarly circumstanced, and the Ministerial party might reasonably have been expected to assert in opposition the views on this subject for which they had incurred the sacrifice of office. Moreover, the position of the House of Assembly itself, in reference to the point which had been raised, was an anomalous one. On the issue, whether or not it was seemly that a certain class of questions

should be dealt with before the dissolution, which would bring into operation a more perfect system of popular representation, that body might be said to be a party to the suit. Its verdict, therefore, in the particular case, could hardly be held to carry with it the authority which, under ordinary circumstances, would attach to the decision of the popular branch of the Legislature. It is further to be observed, that the Legislative Council, by the terms of their address in reply to the speech from the throne which I transmitted in my Despatch No. 5, of the 15th instant, had virtually expressed their approval of the policy adopted by the Administration.

10. Under these circumstances, when the Members of the Executive Council informed me that they were prepared to ask the judgment of the country on the policy of the postponement of the Clergy Reserve and Seigniorial Tenure questions, which they had adopted with my full approval and sanction, I did not think that I should be justified in refusing to act on the advice tendered by them, and to dissolve Parliament for this purpose; and having obtained from the Law Officers of the Crown a joint opinion in favour of the legality of the course recommended to me, I summoned the House of Assembly to the Council Chamber in the usual manner, and delivered the speech, of which the copy is herewith enclosed.—I have, &c.

(Signed)   ELGIN AND KINCARDINE.
The Duke of Newcastle, &c., &c.

Enclosure in No. 2.

Honourable Gentlemen of the Legislative Council.
Gentlemen of the Legislative Assembly.

When I met you at the commencement of the present session, I expressed the hope that you would proceed without delay to pass such a law in reference to the period appointed for introducing the amended franchise, as would have enabled me to bring at once into operation those important measures affecting the representation of the people in Parliament, which were adopted by you with singular unanimity last session. Having been disappointed in this expectation, I still consider that it is due to the people of the province, and most respectful to the decision of the Legislature, that I should take such steps as are in my power to give effect to the law by which the Parliamentary representation of the people is augmented, before calling the attention of Parliament to questions on which the public mind has been long agitated, and the settlement of which it is most desirable to effect in such a manner as will be most likely to secure for it the confidence of the people.

I have come, therefore, to meet you on the present occasion for the purpose of proroguing this Parliament with a view to an immediate dissolution.

I shall comment but briefly on the foregoing papers. I can readily believe that passages in my letter to Sir John Pakington might be cited as justifying *suspicions* as to my intentions regarding secularization. I was not of opinion that in discussing the Clergy Reserve question with the Imperial Ministers I was called upon to express my individual opinions, or even those of the administration of which I was a member. I contended that as between England and Canada it was a question of constitutional right, and that the soundest policy was to adhere strictly to the one point, the repeal of the Imperial Act. The policy which my opponents preferred would probably have caused the disruption of the Reform party a couple of years sooner, and, judging from events, might have postponed the repeal of the Clergy Reserves Act for a long period of years. I can hardly believe that after reading the foregoing statement of facts it will be contended that either Mr. Baldwin or Mr. Lafontaine opposed the reopening of the question, or sought to maintain the Imperial settlement. Mr. Baldwin voted for the declaration that no religious denomination had any vested interests to prevent future legislation. It is now a matter of indifference as to whether our policy was right or wrong, but even those who think that we were wrong in the mode which we adopted, under circumstances of considerable difficulty, should at least refrain from charging us with being opposed to the secularization of the Clergy Reserves. My old surviving friends will I am sure bear in mind that the motto of the old Toronto *Examiner* was, in the darkest period of our history, " Responsible Government and the Voluntary Principle," the motto of the party of which Mr. Baldwin was the recognized leader and from which neither he nor I ever wavered. With regard to the position taken in 1854, that such questions as the Clergy Reserves and the Seigniorial Tenure ought only to be dealt with by the Reformed Parliament, I rest my justification on English practice on the occasion of their Reform acts, but Lord Elgin has put the case of his Ministers so ably in his despatch that I need not add a word. On the other points of difference, such as the right of Roman Catholics to separate schools, to Acts of incorporation for their charitable and educational institutions, and to money grants in aid so long as such grants were given at all, I need only observe that my opinions are unchanged, but I have no complaint to make as to their having been misrepresented as they have been in the case of the Clergy Reserves.]

In the Parliament elected in 1851, there were occasional evidences of a disposition, on the part of the Liberal Opposition, to coalesce with the Conservative Opposition to embarrass the Government. The number inclined to take this course was still small; but the publication of the votes was, of course, not without its effect in shaking confidence. The minority on the sectarian school clause was small, eleven to forty-six; but it is worthy of note that of the eleven, seven were Conservatives and four advanced Liberals. In 1853 the Earl of Elgin paid a visit of some months to England, returning in 1854, charged with the negotiation of a treaty of reciprocity with the United States. As a curious instance of the errors into which writers of history fall, Withrow charges the Ministry with deferring the meeting of Parliament until the 13th June, because they were "conscious of waning influence," although, in the very same page, it is correctly stated that the treaty was only signed on the 5th June, exactly eight days before the time fixed for the meeting; and although the Governor-General had been some months absent, engaged, as I likewise was, both in England and Washington, in the service of the country.

THE GAVAZZI RIOT.

On the preceding page of the same history, there is a statement which, when first read in Withrow, was wholly new to me. Referring to the memorable Gavazzi riot in Montreal in 1853 it is asserted by Withrow that "this tragical occurrence caused intense excitement throughout the country; as the Government failed to make any very rigorous investigation into the affair, the Protestant population strongly denounced the Hincks administration, and transferred their allegiance to Mr. Brown, who was regarded as the most eminent champion of Protestants in the Assembly." To what extent the unfortunate calamity in question may have influenced public opinion, it is of course impossible for me to say, but I can well believe that it was taken advantage of by those who claimed to be the especial champions of Protestantism. It is, however, most unjust to make the administration of the day the scape-goat for the follies of those who brought Gavazzi to Montreal and Quebec, and of those who molested him after he had come. The riot took place in Montreal, the Government was in Quebec. The regiment on duty, and which fired without orders, had only been a few days in Canada. A Court of Enquiry was immediately ordered, and the regiment was soon after transferred to Bermuda. The administration of the day were no more responsible than Mr. Withrow himself for the contretemps, and if it produced the effect which he alleges it did, it affords a curious instance of the misleading influence of religious prejudice. As I have noticed the passage in Withrow relating to the Gavazzi riot, I must express my dissent from another statement which reflects on a gentleman, then Mayor of Montreal, who was present for the express purpose of protecting the congregation of Zion Church from a threatened attack. The gentleman referred to, the late Senator Wilson, positively denied at the time that he ever gave any order to fire, and though the charge was freely made at the time, there was never the slightest ground for it in the opinion of impartial and intelligent men, and for the following reason: It was alleged that the Mayor or some one else cried out "Fire!" Now the military word of command is "Ready, present," and not "Fire," and it never was pretended that any officer gave such a command or that he ever received any request from the Mayor to give it. The firing was, I am persuaded, quite accidental, one man having discharged his piece from misapprehension, and others having followed his example until the officers threw themselves in front, and struck up the firelocks.

The intention of the Government had been to limit the business of the session of 1854 to the legislation required to give effect to the Reciprocity Treaty, and to bring into active operation an Act already passed, extending the franchise, but which did not come into operation until the beginning of the following year. It seemed in accordance with constitutional usage not to proceed to legislate on such important questions as the Clergy Reserves and the Seigniorial question with a House of Assembly which had been pronounced by a two-thirds majority of both Houses to be an inadequate representation of the people. An amendment affirming the propriety of proceeding at once to legislate on these questions was carried by a majority of 42 to 29, the said majority being chiefly composed of Conservatives, with about 15 advanced Liberals from Upper and Lower Canada.

The dissolution of Parliament followed, and the result was the return in Upper Canada of three distinct parties, Ministerialists,

Conservatives and advanced Liberals, who took the name of Clear Grits, by which they were long and are still designated. Of the three parties the Ministerialists were the most numerous. In Lower Canada there were the same divisions, but the Ministerialists outnumbered the combined forces of the Conservatives and the party generally termed Rouges. When the Parliament met it became apparent from the first divisions that the Ministers had not the confidence of the House, and they at once tendered their resignations, whereupon the Governor-General sent for the leader of the Opposition and asked his advice as to the formation of a new Cabinet.

THE COALITION OF 1854.

He at once applied to Mr. Morin, the leader of the Lower Canada majority, for his assistance. The result of the conferences which took place was to satisfy all those who took part in them that there was no essential difference of opinion between them as to the measures to be carried. The Conservatives had for some time back made no secret of their willingness to be guided by the elections as to the mode of settling the Clergy Reserve question, which was the only one causing much embarrassment in Upper Canada. Being of opinion that the combination of parties by which the new Government was supported, presented the only solution of the difficulty caused by a coalition of parties holding no sentiments in common, a coalition which rarely takes place in England, I deemed it my duty to give my support to that Government during the short period that I continued in Canadian public life.

[I shall insert here the letter addressed to me by Mr. Baldwin, not then in public life, approving of the course which I had felt it my duty to take:—

SPADINA, 22nd Sept., 1854.

MY DEAR SIR,—It is not easy for persons to satisfy themselves fully as to what they would themselves have done under a given combination of circumstances in which they have not been placed, and certainly in no department of human affairs is this more true than in politics. The materials with which one has to deal are so various, the prejudices to encounter often so violent (and not unfrequently unjust in proportion to their violence,) that the public man who boldly affirms in a spirit of condemnation, that had he been in the position of another he would have done one thing and not have done another, must be either deficient in experience, or in judgment, or reckless of assertion. If, therefore, by its being "on all sides said that I would never consent to a coalition," it is meant, in that way, to draw a contrast between us to your prejudice, all that I can say is, that those who undertake thus to speak for me, undertake to do so far more positively than I could presume to do myself. For, however disinclined myself to adventure upon such combinations, they are unquestionably, in my opinion, under certain circumstances, not only justifiable but expedient, and even necessary. The Government of the country *must* be carried on. It *ought* to be carried on with vigor. If that can be done in no other way than by mutual concessions and a coalition of parties, they become necessary. And those who, under such circumstances, assume the arduous duty of becoming parties to them, so far from deserving the opprobrium that is too frequently and often too successfully heaped upon them, have, in my opinion, the strongest claims upon public sympathy and support. You have expressed yourself most anxious for my opinion. I feel therefore that I should fail in doing by you what, under similar circumstances, I should expect from you, were I to omit applying the foregoing remarks to the particular transaction which has given occasion to them; with respect to which, then I add without reserve that, in my opinion, you appear to have acted in this matter with judgment and discretion in the interest at once of your party and your country.

   Believe me to be, my dear Sir,
           Yours truly,
    (Signed,)   Robert Baldwin.
Hon. Francis Hincks, M.P.P.]

Although absent for about 14 years, commencing in 1855, I watched the course of events in Canada with unabated interest. It was a gratification to me during the period of my residence in the tropics to receive a deputation of gentlemen commissioned by the Government to enquire as to the best means of extending commercial intercourse between Canada and the West Indies and to have been able to aid in obtaining from British Guiana a promise of co-operation towards the establishment of a line of steamers between a Canadian port and the principal British West Indian Colonies. Before the period of my return the antagonism between Upper and Lower Canada on the subject of the provision in the Union Act for equality of representation in the Legislature had led the contending parties to seek a solution of the difficulty in Confederation.

AN HISTORIAN CORRECTED.

When referring to a question that for many years engaged a large share of public attention, I feel that I may, without impropriety, avail myself of the opportunity to disprove a very serious personal charge made against me in Garneau's history, and very much exaggerated owing to the incorrect translation of the French by Andrew Bell. After referring to the clause in the Union Act of 1840, which provided that the Canadian Legislative Chambers should not have power to change the number of representatives without the consent of two-thirds of the members, the translator proceeds :—

"But one of the Provincial Ministers of Upper Canada, Mr. Hincks, visiting London in 1854, took occasion to get a law passed making members for our Upper Chamber elective (merely) in order to get the restrictive clause noted above annulled by the Imperial Parliament."

In a note there is the following explanation :—

"Mr. Morin, then a member of the Hincks administration, assures me that he was not made privy to such a limitation being intended by his colleagues, nor did he at all know about that change so important in itself to French-Canadians, till he was informed of it by the newspapers."

Mr. Bell's ignorance of French is only equalled by his ignorance of Canadian history. The Act referred to was passed in pursuance of an address from the Canadian Assembly, but the charge as made by Garneau, is an utter fabrication. I could have made precisely the same statement as Mr. Morin with equal truth. I was not in England when the bill was passed, and was never consulted on the subject, and if Mr. Garneau, before publishing a most offensive charge against me, who was absent, had taken the trouble to search the Lords' journals he would have found that the clause referred to was not in the bill as originally introduced by the Duke of Newcastle, but was proposed as an amendment in committee. I have ascertained that a Canadian gentleman who happened to be in England at the time, and who was present in the House of Lords, suggested the amendment to a Peer of his acquaintance, and got him to obtain the concurrence of the Lords to it. Although my interference in such a matter would have been a breach of faith to my colleagues, the gentleman to whom I have referred had a perfect right to make the suggestion. Mr. Turcotte has likewise noticed the repeal of the clause in question, but was too just to hazard a serious charge without proof. He says:—"We are yet ignorant who were the enemies of Lower Canada who suggested this change." To the student of our past history the success of Confederation must appear almost a marvel. It has lasted ten years without serious opposition; indeed, it has been a matter of controversy between rival political parties to which the credit of bringing it about justly belongs. And, yet, it is not quite 40 years since Lords Durham and Sydenham were persuaded that the English population would never again tolerate the authority of a House of Assembly in which the French should possess or even approximate to a majority. The present House of Assembly of Quebec is composed of much the same classes as the old House of Assembly of Lower Canada, and the questions on which the two races are most likely to differ are precisely those which under our constitution have to be dealt with by the Local Legislature. I can hardly doubt that I have long ere this exhausted your patience. The subject must, I fear, be dry and uninteresting to the general public, but it seems to be desirable that the history of those conflicts which secured for the Canadian people that admirable system of self-government which both of the political parties unite in eulogizing should be impressed on the memory of all classes of the people. I will conclude with an expression of my best wishes for the prosperity of your society.

The following should have been inserted on page 16, at the end of the notice of the Hon. R. Baldwin:—

[During my temporary residence in the tropics a work was published in Canada, entitled "Portraits of British Americans by W. Notman, with biographical sketches edited by Fennings Taylor," to which I would have referred in the lecture had it been possible. In the introduction to that work it is stated to have been Mr. Notman's desire that "the sketches should be written fairly and impartially," and accordingly he selected "a gentleman whose duties did not necessarily bring him into confidential intercourse with any member or estate of the Government," but who had "enjoyed fair opportunities of observing the course of public events," and possessed "the habit of equable impartiality that is almost inseparable from official life." The author of the biographies, Mr. Fennings Taylor, has never been charged with writing under the influence of political bias, and most assuredly his sympathies had never been enlisted on the side of politics with which Mr. Baldwin was identified. I should have been glad to have been able to quote at some length from Mr. Fennings Taylor's sketches of "one whose patriotism was as conspicuous for its purity as his character was for its truth," but that is impossible under the circumstances. I avail myself, however, of two interesting records: One, a speech delivered by Mr. Baldwin on the occasion of a charge made against him in connection with his mission to the armed insurgents who were approaching Toronto, on the 5th December, 1837, and the other, his farewell speech after his defeat in the North Riding of York, in 1851. On the latter, I need not offer a single comment. A few remarks may not be out of place on the speech describing Mr. Baldwin's mission to the insurgents. I shall quote Withrow's report as a fair specimen of what I admit to have been the most current version. "The Governor to gain time sent Robert Baldwin and Dr. Rolph, who had hitherto concealed his treason, with a flag of truce, to enquire their demands. The answer was independence, and a written answer was required within an hour." The foundation of the above version is a narrative of Mr. William Lyon Mackenzie, prepared at Navy Island, and intended, if I may use the expression, for the United States market. Mr. Fennings Taylor declared in 1865, that Mr. Baldwin's speech, "set the question for ever at rest," and yet in 1876 Mr. Withrow gives Mr. Mackenzie's version without noticing Mr. Baldwin's. Had the two versions been placed in juxtaposition, I should not have deemed it necessary to notice either. As I have felt it necessary to notice Mr. Withrow's history, I desire to state here in justice to that gentleman, that I have not discovered any tendency to partiality in his history, and that I do not doubt that his numerous errors have been unintentional. He has compiled a great deal from McMullen's history, a work creditable to its author, under the circumstances which he has himself stated, when pleading in defence for short comings his " peculiar position." He "possessed no literary leisure," and if, as I presume to have been the case, he prepared his work at Brockville, where it was published, he could not have had access to a good library. He invites corrections of his errors in view of a second edition, which I fear he was not encouraged to publish. I will here glance at a few errors in Withrow, none of any great consequence, but in all which he has followed McMullen as closely as possible. Lord Dalhousie is said "to have been appointed Governor-General of India," and to have " won merited distinction by his vigorous administration." The Canadian Governor to whom reference is made, was never Governor-General of India, but was Commander-in-Chief in India, in which capacity he had nothing to do with Administration. In giving the list of the Ministry of 1841, Withrow follows McMullen in omitting the name of the Hon. H. H. Killaly. In referring to the change of Ministry in 1842, McMullen made the absurd mistake of stating that "Mr. Sherwood gave place to Mr. Aylwin," the latter being a lawyer practising in Quebec, and the former Solicitor-General for Upper Canada. The Hon. James E. Small, of Toronto, succeeded Mr. Sherwood. It was on McMullen's authority that Withrow stated that I became Inspector-General at that time, whereas I had joined the Government previous to the change. When the Lafontaine-Baldwin administration was formed in 1848, it was composed, says Withrow, of 4 French and 4 British members. McMullen, though himself incorrect, says that it was composed of 8 of British origin and 4 of French. The French Canadian names are given correctly, but Withrow overlooked the fact that there were 2 British names from Lower Canada, Leslie and Aylwin; while there were only 5 in Upper Canada. The cause of that was the decision arrived at that in future the Solicitors-General should not have seats in the Cabinet, but as Mr.

Aylwin had already been in the Council in 1842, he was again sworn in. Withrow omits the names of the Hon. Messrs. Sullivan and Price, and includes Mr. Blake, who was never a member of the Executive Council, although Solicitor-General. In this instance, Withrow has followed McMullen literally as to the names, but has reduced the number by 4. The foregoing errors I cite to show how closely Withrow has followed McMullen, and although the errors are of trifling importance, they are on points where accuracy would be desirable.

" The Hon. member for Hamilton had thought to drag into the discussion allusion to a matter that was personal to himself," (referring to a transaction which had been frequently urged against Mr. Baldwin, as something derogatory to his public character, and of a nature to disqualify him from holding a situation in the government of his country). " However little that matter had to do with the question before the house, he had yet no objection to enter upon it. He would beg to recall to the mind of the Hon. and gallant member for Hamilton that his (Mr. B's) share in that transaction was not a matter of choice with him, but was in a manner forced upon him. He had, indeed, as the Hon. and gallant member affirmed, gone out with a flag of truce to the armed men who had approached Toronto; but at whose instance? (Hear, hear.) It was at the personal desire, and upon the urgent solicitation of the panic-stricken government of Upper Canada, which came to him in the person of the High Sheriff, to request his interference to stop the deluded men who were approaching the city. He complied, and went out with a flag of truce. He was sent back for some evidence from the head of the government that he really came to them in the character and with the authority he pretended to have. And what was the return he received at the hands of the very man who sent him out? Sir Francis Head, through the same functionary, refused to give him a single line to shew that he had really gone out under his sanction; and this humiliating refusal he was compelled to return and announce to those before whom he had but recently appeared as a party clothed with the authority of the government. Sir Francis Head had not the magnanimity to avow his own act.

This was the position in which he had been placed before his country by that man who was the idol of the Hon. and learned member. He (Mr. B.) was made to appear in a most equivocal light, and as a man of bad faith, who was trifling with the very lives of his fellow-men under false pretences. And this was the man at whose call he was expected to take up arms! (Hear.) He had acted then as he would now under similar circumstances, and if condemned by that House, which he did not fear, his own heart would sustain him. His country, which had honored him with its confidence, would not condemn him. He had often been assailed upon this point. He had been held up as a rebel and a traitor—not by the Hon. and gallant member, but by the ribald press which was the organ of his party, and whose chief business it appeared to be to heap calumny and abuse in every form that ingenuity could devise, upon their political opponents. But he cared not for this ribald abuse. He passed it over as unworthy of notice. He thanked God that he had a reputation, and he was perfectly willing to rest that reputation upon the verdict his country would pass upon the passages in his career upon which he had been most assailed. (Hear, hear.) Notwithstanding all the abuse which had assailed him in his own country, which had been repeated against him in the mother country, and spread throughout Europe, what was the result? He had had the honor of being appointed to offices of high confidence by three different representatives of his sovereign, and of having these appointments sanctioned by the Sovereign herself, and that confidence continued to him by a fourth representative of the Sovereign, the present head of the Provincial Government. This was his justification—this his best defence against the taunts of his enemies."

NORTH RIDING—THE DECLARATION.

The Returning Officer having, from the hustings outside, declared the state of the poll, and the return of Mr. Hartman, a desire was intimated to adjourn to the adjoining Court House, to hear what was to be said. This being concurred in, those present, to the number of 100, moved into the Court House, and Mr. Baldwin, followed by Mr. Hartman, ascended a sort of elevated desk. Mr. Baldwin first addressed the meeting. He said the audience had just heard the declaration of a fact that severed the political tie which had, for the last eleven years, connected him with the North Riding of York. It might be said, and no doubt was said by many, that he ought to have withdrawn from the representation of the Riding, rather than contest it under the circumstances which led to the result just announced. He did not view the matter in that light. He felt that a strong sense of duty required him to take a different course, and not to take on himself the responsibility of originating the disruption of a bond which they had formed and repeatedly renewed, between him and the electors of the North Riding. So far as he was able impartially to review the course he had hitherto, and especially for the last four years, pursued, he could see no change in himself, nothing which should have induced them to withdraw a confidence repeatedly expressed at former elections. All circumstances duly considered, he could not recall any act of importance which he had performed, or for which he was responsible, that his sense of duty to his country did not require, or, at least, did not justify. In the course of the canvass just ended, he had frequent opportunities of explaining his views to those who sustained, and occasionally to those who opposed him. It was unnecessary for him then to repeat those views; but he felt it due to his own sense of right, and to the opinions of his friends, to say that, under present circumstances, he saw no reason to withhold a sincere re-assertion of them. In his own mind he could find nothing that would justify him under all the circumstances, in pursuing a different course from that which he had taken. He had the satisfaction of knowing that there were intelligent men of a noble spirit in this Riding who concurred with him—staunch friends of former days, who had on the recent occasion given him their assistance and votes, in the face of, as the result showed, very discouraging circumstances. Principles so approved in his own mind, and so supported by such friends, he could not abandon. Until constitutionally advised to the contrary by the votes of the majority, he felt bound to believe that what he had always supported, what his constituents had frequently affirmed at former elections—what he still believed to be right—what he knew to be still sustained by men of valuable character, was also still concurred in by a majority at least of his constituents. He believed, indeed, that his successful opponent did not differ from him in his view of his (Mr. Baldwin's) position. Under those circumstances he felt he would not be justified in accepting any evidence of a change in the minds of his constituents less doubtful than that of their own recorded votes. It could not now be said of him in leaving, that he had abandoned them. These considerations had impelled him not to shrink from the ordeal of a contest, nor from the announcement now made of its result, however discouraging that result might be considered. It only remained for him now to return his cordial thanks, first and most especially to the staunch friends who in the face of disheartening circumstances had manfully recorded their votes for him, and actively assisted him at the polls and otherwise. To these he felt he could not adequately express his obligations. He would also say that his acknowledgements were due to those who had been his supporters on former occasions, not excepting out of this number his successful rival, for the kindness he had met with among them, and for the courteous manner to himself personally, in which the opposition to him had been conducted. They would part, but part in friendship. They had withdrawn their political confidence from him, and he was now free from responsibility to them. There were among the points of difference between him and their member elect, some not unimportant principles, but although he could not without some alarm observe a tendency which he considered evil, still to all of them personally, he wished the utmost prosperity and happiness they could desire. To his friends, then, of the North Riding, gratefully and not without regret, to his opponents without any feeling of unkindness, he would now say, FAREWELL.

www.ingramcontent.com/pod-product-compliance
Lightning Source LLC
Chambersburg PA
CBHW020311090426
42735CB00009B/1306